Mental Health Services for Minority Ethnic Children and Adolescents

Child and Adolescent Mental Health Series

Written for professionals, and parents, these accessible, evidence-based resources are essential reading for anyone seeking to understand and promote young people's mental health. Drawing on the work of FOCUS, a multidisciplinary project based at the Royal College of Psychiatrists' Research Unit, each title in the series brings together practical and policy-level suggestions with up-to-the-minute analysis of research.

also in the series

Deliberate Self-Harm in Adolescence
Claudine Fox and Professor Keith Hawton
ISBN 1 84310 237 4

FOCUS

Mental Health Services for Minority Ethnic Children and Adolescents

Edited by Mhemooda Malek and Carol Joughin

Foreword by Kedar Nath Dwivedi

The Royal Institute of Psychiatrists' Research Unit

Jessica Kingsley Publishers
London and New York

First published in the United Kingdom in 2004
by Jessica Kingsley Publishers Ltd
116 Pentonville Road
London N1 9JB, England
and
29 West 35th Street, 10th fl.
New York, NY 10001-2299, USA

www.jkp.com

Copyright © The Royal College of Psychiatrists 2004
Foreword copyright © Kedar Nath Dwivedi 2004

Library of Congress Cataloging in Publication Data
A CIP catalog record for this book is available from the Library of Congress

British Library Cataloguing in Publication Data
A CIP catalogue record for this book is available from the British Library

ISBN 1 84310 236 6

Printed and Bound in Great Britain by
Athenaeum Press, Gateshead, Tyne and Wear

Contents

Part One

Part Two

Foreword

There is now a growing emphasis on evidence-based practice and clinical governance. According to the Department of Health, clinical governance is 'a framework through which NHS organisations are accountable for continuously improving the quality of their services and safeguarding high standards of care by creating an environment in which excellence in clinical care will flourish'. In such a context, this publication by the Royal College of Psychiatrists is extremely useful and very timely. It aims to help improve the provision of culturally sensitive child and adolescent mental health services for minority ethnic families. Not only child and adolescent mental health professionals but also service managers and commissioners will find this publication helpful, concise, clear and practical.

The chapters have been written by a number of authors with expertise in their respective fields and therefore each chapter reflects the individual's approach. Added value has been achieved by Mhemooda Malek visiting a variety of services, contacting and discussing with key professionals and opinion leaders, conducting a survey of commissioners and managers and also distilling the contributions from a seminar for the voluntary sector organised for the purpose. Thus, a great deal of effort has gone into grounding this important work with reality at grass roots level, so that it is more likely to lead to right action.

Anyone working in this field is fully aware of the enormous gap between words and action. For example, in Northampton, a group of dedicated professionals initiated an excellent and pioneering mental health work with children and adolescents from minority ethnic communities but as soon as the local Primary Care Trust took on its commissioning responsibilities, they discontinued the project and killed it off prematurely. This happened in spite of loud and clear feedback to the contrary from users, providers and multi-agency planners.

In most parts of the country, however, there is rising awareness of the issues because of recent publications and the efforts of some groups and agencies interested in this theme. There are also some good practices beginning to emerge; a few of them have already been outlined in this volume. However, there is still a long way to go and this publication will be of immense help in that journey.

Kedar Nath Dwivedi

Acknowledgements

FOCUS would like to thank the many individuals who gave their time freely to advise and contribute to the development of this report. We have received input from so many people that we apologise to those we may have missed. A special thanks go to the child and adolescent service managers and commissioners who contributed in such an open and honest way to the survey on current planning and provision.

Advisory Group

Dr Matthew Hodes, Senior Lecturer, Academic Unit of Child and Adolescent Psychiatry, Imperial College School of Medicine, St Mary's Campus, Norfolk Place, London W2 1PG.

Dr Usha Jayarajan, Clinical Psychologist, Birmingham Children's Hospital, Steelhouse Lane, Birmingham B4 6NH.

Dr Begum Maitra, Consultant Child and Family Psychiatrist, Lower Clapton Child and Family Consultation Service, 36 Lower Clapton Road, London E5 0PQ.

Ms Dinah Morley, Deputy Director, YoungMinds, 102–108 Clerkenwell Road, London EC1M 5SA.

Dr Paul Ramchandani, MRC Research Fellow, University of Oxford Department of Psychiatry, Warneford Hospital, Warneford Lane, Headington, Oxford OX3 7JX.

Other contributors to this book:

Reena Ali, Bill Bulloten, Meera Chandran, Melvyn Davis, Neil Daws, Yesim Deveci, Sue Dodd, Kedar Dwivedi, Raina Fatch, Shila Khan, Jenny Mahimbo, Muhamad Mboowa, Anne McGrath, Phillip Messant, Anne Miller, Helen Minnis, Anula Nikapota, Jude Sellen, Tim Spafford, Andrew Starr, Matesebia Tadesse, Jenny Taylor, Panos Vostanis, Amy Weir.

Preface

The mental health of children and adolescents is recognised as playing a vital role in enabling individuals to achieve their potential, sense of well-being and make positive contributions to wider society. The range of mental health disciplines that aim to address mental health difficulties are not without controversy with reference to how mental health needs are understood and addressed. One of the areas in which this is most apparent is in the context of ethnicity. The issues raised include questions about the:

- definitions and meaning of ethnicity
- relationship between mental health and ethnicity
- relevance of mental health disciplines evolved in the West, to understanding and addressing the mental health needs of those from a diversity of cultures
- reliability and validity of available studies looking at mental health in the context of ethnicity
- extent to which services address the needs of clients from minority ethnic groups.

This publication aims to address the above issues. A range of approaches have been used to bring together relevant material. Available literature, though relatively sparse, has highlighted some important issues and debates about 'ethnicity', links between 'mental health and ethnicity' and issues that need to be considered in providing services that are relevant to this group. Papers contributed by CAMHS practitioners provide invaluable insights into academic as well as practical considerations that need to be taken into account. The survey of CAMHS gives a snapshot of how the issue of mental health and ethnicity is addressed by statutory provision.

The importance of work undertaken in the voluntary sector is highlighted through available literature and data generated through a seminar, organised as part of this project.

These approaches have greatly facilitated achieving the initial aim of producing a comprehensive document that addresses a range of key issues, relevant to the mental health of children and young people from minority ethnic groups.

Introduction

Mhemooda Malek

Ensuring that all children have equal access to high quality health care, including mental health care, is fundamental to the NHS Plan (2000). Core principles of the NHS Plan highlight that the National Health Service of the 21st century must be responsive to the needs of different groups and individuals within society and challenge discrimination on the grounds of age, gender, ethnicity, religion, disability and sexuality. The NHS must be responsive to the different needs of different populations and services must be provided that are tailored to individual needs. Services will be assessed against a range of performance standards which include fair access to services, effective and appropriate delivery of health care, and high quality experiences of patients and carers.

Over the last five to ten years a range of information and resources have been produced which address the mental health needs of adults from minority ethnic groups. Although many of the messages that arise from this body of literature are transferable and may be used to inform the development of child and adolescent mental health services (CAMHS) in the United Kingdom, it is apparent from the slowness of CAMHS to review and adapt service provision for this group of children, which will meet the standards described in the NHS Plan, that additional information is required.

The intention of this publication is to bring together information relevant to the mental health of young people from minority ethnic groups. The purpose of highlighting key issues and debates is to assist in the making of informed decisions about ethnicity, minority ethnic groups and the development of approaches that aim to be culturally competent.

The contents are not intended to be, in any way, prescriptive and the dangers of doing so are highlighted in a number of texts (Nikapota, 2001; Patel 2000). Understanding and addressing the mental health needs of minority ethnic groups requires recognition of the diversity of individual needs and cultures, assuming a uniformity of experience is unlikely to be helpful. This report aims to provide background information to encourage both commissioners and practitioners to reflect on the appropriateness of their services for children and adolescents from minority ethnic groups. There is a tension in current thinking about the most appropriate approach to adopt in providing services for minority ethnic groups and this tension is reflected in the breadth of this report. Understanding individuals and their cultural context is likely to be a more productive approach than generalising on the basis of stereotypical approaches.

In the first three chapters of this report we have attempted to explore the contribution of all these approaches to the development of knowledge and practice. Chapter 4 explores the key issues that affect access to and provision of services that are culturally sensitive as well as highlighting the key role of commissioning in developing appropriate services.

This report is by no means comprehensive in its coverage. For example, the mental health needs of young people from minority ethnic groups in particular systems, such as juvenile justice and looked after by social services, have not been covered in any depth as originally intended. Site visits undertaken as a part of the development of this report highlighted a significant amount of activity in addressing the needs of particular groups such as these, but much of this work remains undocumented.

Early discussions with professionals about the kind of resource they would find useful elicited responses that could be described largely as being at opposite ends of the spectrum. Those already familiar with mental health and ethnicity said they would not find yet another document highlighting the 'basics' (such as defining ethnicity and differing perceptions of mental health) to be of use. Those less familiar with this area wanted precisely this kind of information. It was perhaps an early indication of the differences in knowledge that exist between professionals and one that is certainly borne out by feedback obtained through the FOCUS survey (see below).

Part Two presents the findings of a small survey that was undertaken by FOCUS in 2001 to gain additional information from commissioners and child and adolescent mental health service managers about their understanding and approaches to service development for children from minority ethnic groups. Data provided by survey respondents indicates that some services are indeed further ahead in achieving cultural competence than others. Difficulties highlighted in achieving this by some services appear to be addressed by others and an apparent gap appears to be the lack of communication in sharing good practice.

The project timescale was May 2001 to February 2002. Within this period we have tried to obtain the broadest possible overview of key issues and practice in relation to child and adolescent mental health services for minority ethnic groups. Three broad methods were applied to gather data and other relevant material.

1. Literature search and identification of relevant initiatives/resources

To inform Chapter 3, which addresses epidemiology, and Chapter 4, which examines the development of services for minority ethnic group children, we sought to identify papers published in the United Kingdom between 1990 and 2001. It would not have been possible to assess the applicability of international studies to the UK within the available timeframe. Assessing the relevance of studies from other countries is important for a number of reasons. In addition to possible differences in the structure and delivery of services and circumstances of minority groups in other countries, there is also the added complexity of discrepancies in how minority groups are defined. Sources used for literature searches were:

- PsychInfo
- Medline
- Internet web searches
- hand searching
- word of mouth.

Search terms included: Multicultural; Ethnic; Culture; Minority Group; Ethnic Group; Race; Racial Groups; Discrimination; Racial and Ethnic Differences; Racism; Black. A significant amount of relevant literature was identified through hand searching and word of mouth. This issue has also been highlighted in recent work commissioned by the NHS Executive (Atkinson *et al.* 2001). The study, *A Systematic Review of Ethnicity and Health Service Access for London,* is not confined to particular age groups and echoes our own conclusions in relation to CAMHS for minority ethnic groups. The NHS study found:

- The number of publications that could be classed as suitable for systematic review were fewer than 10 in most of the areas considered, with 15 considered suitable for mental health.

- A substantial body of research was found to exist but was mostly policy-led, owned by local institutions and not widely disseminated.

- There was an emphasis on short-termism, with much innovation being project-based and disappearing when funding periods came to an end.

Studies looking at the mental health of minority ethnic groups in the UK have largely focused on adults and, in some cases, in the context of broader health needs and provision. Literature focusing on young people in this context is sparse and some of the available studies have subsumed young people within observations that encompass a range of age groups. Nevertheless, some of the issues highlighted in such studies have relevance for mental health provision for young people and, where appropriate, have been included in the text.

In the absence of sufficient relevant literature that could be accessed through the usual search strategies on medical databases, it was considered important to adopt a range of methods to identify material. Such information was considered necessary to inform the structure of this project. Informal contact was made with a number of professionals from the early stages of developing this work. There was no systematic approach to identifying individuals, or initiatives. Some were known through the work they have published and others were identified through word of mouth. The purpose of this exercise was to:

- obtain feedback about current issues relating to mental health of young people from minority ethnic groups
- identify relevant research and other work.

This approach proved invaluable in identifying relevant literature that was either unpublished, work in progress or material that would be unlikely to be identified through formal literature search strategies.

2. Survey of practice

A telephone survey was undertaken of 13 commissioners and 14 CAMHS managers (Tier 3 services). This is described in detail in Part Two and relevant findings from the survey are also included in Part One.

3. Seminar on work being undertaken in the voluntary sector

No overview of mental health services for minority ethnic groups would be complete without highlighting the significant contribution of services in the voluntary sector. Within the available timescale for this programme of work, it was decided that the best approach to facilitating feedback and discussion with voluntary sector staff working with minority ethnic groups would be via a seminar (described in Appendix I).

Defining minority ethnic groups

The complexities of defining ethnicity are presented in Chapter 1 and should be taken into account in considering references to particular minority ethnic groups. Much research and service provision defines ethnic categories based on those used in the Census where they are defined on the basis of skin colour, country of origin or both. The general use of the term 'minority ethnic groups' in this publication refers to all groups who are in a minority as compared to the overall majority population of Britain. Wherever possible, the unnecessary use of broad categories such as 'Black' or 'South Asian' is avoided. However, a significant amount of the literature included here does refer to broad categories and lacks clarity as to the particular groups encompassed. Consequently the use of all-encompassing terms has been unavoidable in reference to some studies.

References

Atkinson, M., Clark, M., Clay, D., Johnson, M., Owen, D. and Szczepura, A. (2001) *Systematic Review of Ethnicity and Health Service Access for London*. University of Warwick: Centre for Health Services Studies.

Nazaroo, J. (1998) 'Genetic, cultural or socio-economic vulnerability? Explaining ethnic inequalities in health.' *Sociology of Health and Illness 20*, 710–730.

NHS (2000) *The NHS Plan: A Plan for Investment. A Plan for Reform*. London: HMSO.

Nikapota, A. (2001) 'Child Psychiatry.' In D. Bhugra and R. Cochrane (eds) *Psychiatry in Multicultural Britain*. London: Gaskell.

Patel, N. (ed) (2000) *Clinical Psychology: 'Race' and Culture: A Training Manual*. London: BPS Books.

Recommendations
FOCUS

Commissioning services

1. Comprehensive commissioning strategies for child and adolescent mental health services need to be developed, implemented and evaluated to ensure that they meet the needs of minority ethnic groups.

2. Health service restructuring should routinely evaluate the impact of new models of service delivery on minority ethnic groups.

3. Appropriate needs assessments are conducted as part of the commissioning process and representatives from minority ethnic groups are involved in this process.

4. Voluntary sector organisations are appropriately involved in the commissioning process.

5. Each locality develops a directory of all agencies and contact names, who provide culturally sensitive services.

CAMHS providers

6. Each CAMHS develops and implements a service delivery strategy for children from minority ethnic groups.

7. Data collection systems are developed to provide accurate and useful information relating to children and adolescents from minority groups.

8. Services review the provision of targeted information (both written and oral) about their services to minority ethnic groups.

9. Intake, assessment and intervention procedures are reviewed to ensure that they take into account the individual needs of children, adolescents, their families and the wider community.

10. Services review the provision and training of interpreters to ensure that best practice is achieved.

11. Training in cultural competence is incorporated into the personal development plans of clinicians and administrative staff.

12. Services are developed and evaluated in collaboration with members of minority ethnic groups.

13. Further research is conducted in order to improve access of, and clinical care provided to, children from minority ethnic groups to CAMHS.

Professional bodies

14. Professional bodies develop explicit frameworks for providing and evaluating cultural competence.

Part One

1 Understanding Ethnicity and Children's Mental Health

Mhemooda Malek

Mental health and ethnicity share some common features. For example, both are complex subjects in their own right, cannot be easily defined, mean different things to different people, are used interchangeably with other terms, and have the capacity to be emotive and confusing. It is useful to outline briefly the definition of mental health in children and adolescents in the context of this report before considering ethnicity and ethnicity in the context of mental health.

The term 'mental health' is often confused with that of mental illness though the two refer to quite different states. Mental health is said to be closely linked to physical health and well-being in general. Kurtz (1996) usefully sums this up as health being the basis for a good quality of life and mental health has an overriding importance in this. Mental health in children and adolescents has been defined (Health Advisory Service 1995) as the ability to:

- develop psychologically, emotionally, intellectually and spiritually

- initiate, develop and sustain mutually satisfying personal relationships

- become aware of others and to empathise with them

- use psychological distress as a developmental process, so that it does not hinder or impair further development.

'Mental illness' encompasses a range of difficulties from relatively minor conditions of stress and anxiety to more severe disorders. This term is often used interchangeably with other terms such as 'mental health difficulties', 'mental disorders' and 'mental health problems'. Mental ill health is divided into three broad categories according to their severity (Health Advisory Service 1995; House of Commons Health Committee 1997):

- **Mental health problems** refer to a broad range of conditions that are relatively minor in severity and considered to be relatively common.

- **Psychiatric disorders** are conditions distinguished by a higher level of distress or disability, can be longer-lasting and less likely to be resolved without professional intervention than are mental health problems.

- **Mental illness** incorporates severe forms of psychiatric disorder and is more likely than psychiatric disorders to require professional intervention.

Defining ethnicity

As with mental health, 'ethnicity' is often used interchangeably with other terms such as 'race', 'culture' and 'ethnic origin'. The term 'race', though still in frequent use, is increasingly acknowledged (Fenton 1999; Smaje 1995) as a concept that:

- lacks scientific validity

- demonstrates a history of being used to create a hierarchy of superior and inferior 'races'

- has attributed physical difference to also mean biological difference between people.

Some writers (Fenton 1999) argue that, precisely because the term is still in frequent use, it cannot be discarded completely. The term has social significance because there are social meanings still attributed to the notion of 'race'; as such it remains an important feature in people's thinking and in the ordering of social relations.

Increasing preference, however, is given to the concept of ethnicity. Unlike 'race' which has come to be associated with physical or biological difference, ethnicity is linked to cultural difference and encompasses a broad range of factors. A major difficulty posed in relation to devising a conclusive definition of ethnicity is that this concept is not static and can be informed by group affiliation as well as individual constructs.

The way ethnicity is perceived and defined is, among other things, influenced by social, political, historical and economic circumstances (Smaje 1995). The concept of ethnicity has no universal or fixed definition; it has different meanings across time, place and people. Recognising ethnicity as a fluid and varied notion, especially in the context of service provision, has gained momentum in the UK over the last decade or so. A number of considerations have been highlighted; particularly relevant to the context of service provision is the distinction between ethnicity as an identity and ethnicity as a category.

Ethnicity as identity

As an identity, ethnicity has been described as a process by which people create and maintain a sense of identity, which they use to distinguish themselves from others (Fenton 1999; Smaje 1995). Individuals may identify with an ethnic group with whom they share a common culture; they may also perceive themselves as having a number of ethnic identities. These may be informed by geographical associations with countries, religious or political belief systems, social circumstances, language, dress codes, skin colour and so on.

Ethnicity is frequently associated with country of origin, though this is only one of a number of factors that inform an individual's ethnic identity. Furthermore, the features that inform ethnic identity in one country are unlikely to be identical in the context of individuals' lives in another country, or indeed in the same country at different points in time and in different regions. Therefore, the way of life in Pakistan may not be a relevant indicator of the beliefs, values and experiences of Pakistanis in England. This is of relevance to mental health because understanding the context of people's lives in their country of origin is unlikely to be sufficient in helping to address their needs within the context of their lives in another country.

Ethnicity as category

As a category ethnicity has been described as the process by which external categories, such as those used in the Census, are created and imposed by others and with which people so categorised may not necessarily identify (Smaje 1995).

Ethnic categories do not in themselves provide information about identity. For example, the category 'African' does not provide details of an individual's religious beliefs, language spoken, country of origin within the continent and so on. Categories such as Indian, African, British and Irish each encompass a broad range of identities. As such they are not in themselves useful if the data required needs to take account of the broader range of factors related to individual ethnic identity. Given that ethnic categories are most frequently used in datasets that inform planning, provision and monitoring of services, it is important to know their limitations and the extent to which they can provide the required information. This is explored in the subsection 'Statistics relating to ethnicity'.

SAME CATEGORY, DIFFERENT IDENTITY

The relationship between ethnic identity and country of origin is also likely to mean different things to different generations who identify themselves as originating from one country. For example, the factors that a first generation migrant from India incorporates in forming an ethnic identity are not necessarily the same as those incorporated by a second or subsequent generation Indian, though both may select the ethnic category 'Indian'.

Development of self-identity

In addition to considerations of group identity, another important dimension that may need to be explored in relation to the mental health of young people from minority ethnic groups is that of self-identity. A recent paper (Bains 2001) considers the effects of migration and cross-cultural issues on the development of self-autonomy and self-identity on second generation young people. The issues highlighted are based on work undertaken with young people of Indian and Bangladeshi origin who were referred for psychotherapy. The issues raised are:

- Children of first generation migrants may experience conflict in developing a cohesive sense of self due to issues relating to cultural identity. In such situations young people's development of a self-identity can arise from the conflict involving the integration of the self in the minority and the self in the majority culture.

- Difficulties experienced in accommodating the demands of two distinct cultures can complicate the process of developing a self-identity.

- Parental experiences of migration can have a significant impact on children's development of a self-identity. Negative experiences in relation to acculturation and quality of life in England may contribute to the conflict felt by young people in developing a cohesive sense of self. The conflict in young people is said to arise from the pressure to acculturate to the country migrated to, while maintaining a cultural identity relating to the country of origin.

- Further complications in the development of a self-identity can arise if:
  - individual members of the family have different levels of affiliation to the culture of the country migrated to
  - the young person perceives this culture as being hostile and rejecting.

The impact of these factors on young people and their experience of participating in therapy are reported as:

- Feelings of confusion in not knowing what they wanted from therapy. The confusion appeared to develop from internal conflict concerning the development of a cultural identity based on a more cohesive sense of self.

- Feelings of anger and hostility arising from not being able to accommodate the demands of two cultures resulted in noticeable feelings of isolation and possibly rejection.

- For some young people, participating in therapy was like accommodating yet another culture – that of psychotherapy.

The insights provided by this study provide a basis for further exploring the factors that impact on the development of self-identity and its impact on mental health in a wider group of young people.

The term 'self-definition', whereby respondents are said to self-identify, is not without constraints, as the term might initially suggest, for example, where respondents are limited to selecting their ethnicity from a set of predetermined categories, or their otherwise more qualitative responses are standardised to fit categories required for administrative purposes.

Who can be defined as a minority ethnic group?

There can be a tendency to see ethnicity as relating to 'minority' groups and in particular those that are seen as 'non-White'. To some extent this is exacerbated by categorisations used in datasets such as the Census (discussed later in this chapter) and is apparent in terminology such as 'minority ethnic groups' and 'majority White groups'. This can create the impression that ethnicity relates to skin colour only and those who are 'White', do not have ethnicity. However, as an identity, ethnicity clearly applies to all people. An important recognition is that some aspects of ethnicity, such as skin colour or country of origin, can play a significant part in the experience of discrimination and disadvantage, whereby some groups are at greater risk than others (see 'Socio-economic factors and mental health' regarding racism, below).

Ethnicity as a variable in research and practice

Researching ethnicity is a complex subject and requires much more data than is currently available through local and national sources such as statistical datasets. Standard scientific criteria may not apply to the measurement of ethnicity and, perhaps due to the methodological problems posed, there is little empirical work currently available in this area

(Nazaroo 1998). If the changing nature of ethnicity is to be given due consideration then it needs to be contextualised and data to be analysed according to the various factors that inform ethnicity such as religion, country of origin, language and so on.

In order to understand the relationship between ethnicity and health, including mental health, it is necessary to theorise ethnicity adequately. This requires recognising ethnicity as both category and identity. At present there is a lack of consistency in the way in which ethnicity is defined in both literature and practice.

Defining ethnicity in CAMHS

Recent studies have examined ethnicity in relation to CAMHS (Hodes *et al.* 1998; Kramer *et al.* 2000). The key points being raised are that within psychiatric research ethnicity is commonly described by:

- physical attributes
- place of birth
- staff perception
- self-definition.

Highly relevant for CAMHS use are a number of related issues:

- place of birth of the young person
- language used at home
- religion
- heterogeneity of parental dyad (as may be represented for children of dual heritage).

The above list should not be seen as exhaustive; other factors may also be relevant in the way they impact on individuals.

The need to be clear about the type of information needed and the purposes for which it is required is apparent. Data needed for administrative purposes is likely to be different to that needed for providing effective clinical interventions. Another consideration relates to the information needs of individual CAMHS, a collection of CAMHS locally and nationally, the Health Authority or Trust and inter-agency work across multidisciplinary teams.

Recording ethnicity

Though the recording of ethnicity is mandatory for some types of provision, there is evidence to suggest that such data can be missing despite this requirement. For example, the recent systematic review of health service access for London (Atkinson *et al.* 2001) found that this data was missing for 40 per cent of hospital admissions. Without this data, it is difficult to assess aspects of service provision such as access and under- or over-representation of particular groups of clients.

It is pertinent to highlight here a recent study of a CAMHS service (Messent and Murrell 2003). The study reports that due to the low rate of recording of client ethnicity, it was not possible to undertake a randomised selection of cases for research purposes. Non-recording was found despite health trust and social services department policies stating that data about client ethnicity should be obtained on first contact. Subsequent discussions about this with clinicians revealed that they were hesitant to implement this policy. Clinicians felt that raising questions about ethnicity was seen as 'shaping' the initial contact in ways that were unhelpful in the development of a therapeutic relationship. Nevertheless, discussion within the team about these misgivings led to the recognition of the need for this data and consideration given to ways of improving its collection. The authors cite this as one of the concrete changes they hoped would occur as a result of undertaking this work.

The need to record a range of relevant information about client ethnicity has been highlighted by two recent studies focusing on CAMHS provision (Jayarajan unpublished; Minnis *et al.* 2003). Jayarajan found information about a family's faith was not being routinely collected by the service (missing in 80% of the cases), suggesting a failure to acknowledge the importance of the family's religious and spiritual beliefs. Discussions with staff revealed an acknowledgement that this information was relevant to the provision of a culturally aware and sensitive service. However, staff felt uncomfortable asking for this information, possibly due to the fact that they did not already know or because they were unable to explain to clients why this information was needed. The discussion resulted in highlighting that client faith could be a significant consideration in ensuring access to the service.

Similarly, Minnis *et al.* found cultural and religious issues were mentioned in some case notes but not explored further with the family. Follow-up discussions with clinicians revealed that such issues had, in fact, been further explored with some families, but had not been recorded. The authors conclude that the non-recording of data is possibly due to the highly structured way in which psychiatrists and allied professionals are trained to perform assessment interviews, covering a standard range of subjects that do not make room for cultural, religious and language/communication issues.

Statistics relating to ethnicity

Statistics play an important role in definitions of ethnicity and in the provision of services that address the needs of minority ethnic groups. One

FOCUS Survey (Part 2): Defining and recording ethnicity in CAMHS

The significant part played by categories based on datasets such as the Census is apparent in the definitions and views given by both sets of survey respondents (commissioners and CAMHS managers). It is also evident in the responses that some services are further ahead than others in addressing the need for information that can be standardised for administrative purposes and richer, more qualitative data needed for clinical intervention.

Services are using a wide range of sources (referrer, parent or child) to collect client ethnicity data. There is a need for services to consider which source is most appropriate. Referrer feedback about client ethnicity may not always be a reliable source.

Data relating to country of origin was collected by all of the services that recorded client ethnicity (12 out of 14). There was no consistent pattern in the nature of other information recorded and the extent to which available sources were relevant and reliable was not clear.

Recommendations

Data collection systems need to be developed to provide accurate and relevant information relating to children and adolescents from minority ethnic groups.

of the most widely known and used sources of statistical information is the Census. The ethnic categories and related information provided in the Census are widely used by services to plan provision and as the basis to collect ethnic monitoring data. Less conspicuously perhaps, these categories can also influence how ethnicity is perceived and defined, particularly in the context of service provision.

Though country of origin and skin colour are only two of a number of dimensions that inform ethnicity, they are the most frequently used in collecting statistical data about individual ethnicity. This is apparent in national sources such as the Census and Labour Force Survey, local sources covering smaller geographical areas such as local authority data, and sources pertaining to particular services such as school population statistics.

That is not to say that statistical data relating to ethnic categories is of no use. However, it is important to be clear about the type of information required and the extent to which available sources can provide this. Particular sources may themselves be refined to accommodate the need to achieve a better picture in relation to ethnicity, as is apparent in the Census.

The Census

The Census has undergone a number of changes in relation to collecting data that relates to ethnicity (see Box 1.1). It is relevant to highlight these briefly because the type of data available has implications for policy, practice and research, including retrospective and comparative work.

It is clear that some efforts have been made to refine the collection of data on ethnicity. The 2001 census should provide more sophisticated data than has been the case previously. Nevertheless, it is important to

Pre-1971

The nationality of individuals was the only data available that related to ethnicity. Nationality is not a reliable indicator of ethnicity. It is possible to be a national of a particular country without actually originating from, or otherwise having an affiliation to, that country.

1971 and 1981

These asked for the country of birth of the respondent and their parents. This data would have picked up the many migrants who came to Britain in the 1950s and 1960s. However, it was still not a reliable indicator of ethnicity and became less so over time given the increasing number of individuals born in the UK but who may consider themselves as having origins in another country.

The main barrier to formulating a question on ethnicity appears to have been the difficulty with generating a question that provided categorical data required by those using it while also addressing the issue of identity from the perspective of respondents (Leech 1989).

1991

Respondents were asked to select from a set of pre-defined categories. The type of information requested was not consistent across the categories provided, relating either to skin colour (e.g. White), country (e.g. Pakistani) or both (Black African). The 'White' category was not broken down into any subcategories, thereby limiting the identification of White minorities.

2001

Pre-defined categories were provided again but with some modifications to those in the 1991 census. The changes include:

- Individual categories that respondents were asked to select were provided under one of five main category

> headings: 'White', 'Mixed', 'Asian or Asian British',
> 'Black or Black British', 'Chinese or other ethnic group'.
>
> - All main headings include the subcategory 'Any Other
>   (background)'. Previously 'Other' was only provided as
>   one overall option.
>
> - The 'White' category included subcategories for the first
>   time, though these are limited to 'British', 'Irish' and
>   'Any other White background'.
>
> - The category 'Mixed' and its subcategories were
>   introduced for the first time.

Box 1.1 Changes in Census data on ethnicity

recognise that this source still remains one of 'ethnicity as category'. The instability and lack of reliability of either self-defined or ascribed ethnicity is said to limit the validity of using ethnicity data in the allocation of resources and in the planning of future services (Bhui *et al.* 1995; Smaje 1995).

Notwithstanding the limitations of available data, it is pertinent to look at what is highlighted in the Census in relation to who the minority groups are and their geographic locations. This has relevance to subsequent sections, in particular those looking at the impact of socio-economic factors and at epidemiology.

Minority ethnic groups in Britain

The 1991 Census indicated that 3 million or 6 per cent of the total population of Britain were members of non-White groups. This figure does not take account of under-enumeration which was proportionately greater among minority ethnic populations and in particular among young Black men (Raleigh and Balarajan 1994).

The Labour Force Survey (which provides population estimates for years other than the Census years) indicates an increase in 1997 and

1998 to 6.4 per cent. However, the reasons for this are not entirely clear. Possible explanations suggested are (Schuman 1999):

- an actual increase due to the higher concentration of minority ethnic groups in the fertile age range and larger family sizes in minority ethnic groups compared to the majority population

- possible changes in recent years in the way that people categorise themselves.

It should also be noted that the Labour Force Survey is based on data collected from private households and excludes some groups such as the prison population, where people from minority ethnic groups are disproportionately over-represented.

The categories used in the 1991 Census were divided into White and non-White groups. 'Ethnic minority' is the term generally used to refer to people who did not tick the 'White' category and therefore to 'non-White' minorities. Figures for the British population by ethnicity are: White 94 per cent; non-White 6 per cent. The 6 per cent who are referred to as 'non-White' are allocated to the following categories:

Black Caribbean	17%
Black African	7%
Black other	6%
Indian	28%
Bangladeshi	5.5%
Pakistani	15.5%
Chinese	5%
Other Asian	6.5%
Other	9.5%

There is no data available from the Census about the numbers of some minority groups such as those of Turkish, Greek, or Middle Eastern origin. Figures for those who have dual heritage are also not available from the 1991 Census but this data has been requested in the 2001 Census. The 'Other' category is likely to encompass many of those who do not identify with the pre-defined categories provided.

Some groups, such as those who are refugees, will cut across a range of the Census categories. In relation to people with refugee status, consideration needs to be given to their needs as migrants from another country as well as their needs arising from being a refugee.

The majority of minority ethnic groups live predominantly in inner city areas and 97 per cent of Britain's non-White population live in England (ONS 1998; Owen 1996).

- The largest concentration of minority ethnic groups is in Greater London; approximately 50 per cent of all minority ethnic groups and less than 10 per cent of the White population live here.

- Inner London has one-third of its population of minority ethnic origin.

- Between them, Greater London, Greater Manchester, West Yorkshire and West Midlands have approximately 75 per cent of the minority ethnic population living there. Less than 25 per cent of the White population lives in these areas.

- People from minority ethnic groups are less likely than White people to live in Wales, Scotland, and in the North East and South West regions of England.

A breakdown of all minority ethnic groups by *region* is presented in Table 1.1.

Individual minority ethnic groups are even more likely to be concentrated in particular areas:

- Caribbeans, Africans and Bangladeshis live predominantly in the Inner London areas.

- Indian communities are predominantly resident in Outer London areas; one-third of the entire Indian Community in England lives here. Significant numbers have also settled in the West Midlands and Leicestershire.

Table 1.1 Minority and majority groups by region of residence (Owen 1996)

Region	White as % of Whites in Great Britain	Minority ethnic groups as % of minority ethnic groups in Great Britain
South East	29.9	56.4
Greater London	*10.3*	*44.8*
West Midlands	9.1	14.1
West Midlands MC	*4.2*	*12.4*
North West	11.6	8.1
Greater Manchester	*4.5*	*4.9*
Merseyside	*2.7*	*0.8*
Yorks & Humberside	8.9	7.2
East Midlands	7.3	6.3
Scotland	9.5	2.1
South West	8.8	2.1
Wales	5.4	1.4
East Anglia	3.8	1.4
North	5.8	1.3
Tyne & Wear	*2.1*	*0.7*
TOTAL	100% (51,843,900)	100% (3,006,500)

- Pakistani communities are mostly resident in the West Midlands and Yorkshire.

- Chinese communities have mostly settled in London, Merseyside and Manchester.

For the migrants who came here in the 1950s and 1960s, choices about geographical residence are likely to have been influenced by employment prospects and requirements. Two other explanations proposed are 'choice' and 'constraint' theories (Lakey 1997; Ratcliffe 1999).

CHOICE

This theory argues that minority ethnic groups may prefer to live in close proximity to others from the same ethnic group. The reasons for this are cited as shared linguistic, cultural and religious beliefs and practices, and support networks.

CONSTRAINT

This theory argues that minority ethnic groups are unable to live in certain areas due to economic status, lack of information about housing opportunities elsewhere, actual discrimination and fear of discrimination.

Figures for Britain's minority ethnic population by age are presented in Figure 1.1.

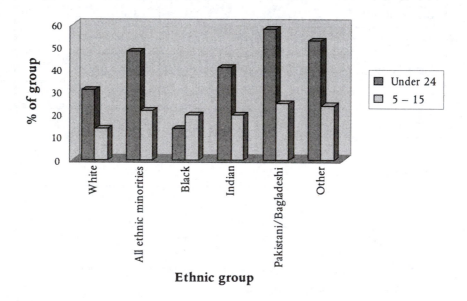

Figure 1.1 Young people in Britain by age and ethnic group, Spring 1997

Ethnic categories in other countries

An important consideration in looking at international research and practice is the possibility that a single term (or category) can have different meanings in different countries. For example, as Senior and Bhopal (1994) point out, the term 'Asian' in Britain is frequently used to refer to people with origins in the Indian Subcontinent. However, in the US 'Asian' is frequently used to refer to those with origins in East and South East Asia. Indeed, in the 2001 UK census, subcategories included under the main category 'Asian or Asian British' are countries from the Indian Subcontinent, while 'Chinese' is a subcategory under the main heading 'Chinese or other ethnic group'.

Some factors to take into account in using ethnic statistics

- The distinction between category and identity.

- The extent to which available statistics usefully highlight health experience of minority ethnic groups.

- National surveys such as the Census and Labour Force surveys are not designed to obtain data that is primarily for the purposes of health research and planning.

- The type of data required and the extent to which available sources can provide this.

Socio-economic factors and mental health

In order to understand the relationship between ethnicity and health, including mental health, it is necessary to recognise wider social inequalities (such as racism and class inequalities) alongside other risk factors (Lloyd 1998; Williams *et al.* 1994). Too narrow a focus on ethnicity can result in the downplaying of significant relationships between mental health, ethnicity and other important variables. Indeed, the risk factors identified as predisposing young people to mental health problems include a range of environmental risks including socio-economic disadvantage, discrimination and family risk factors that incorporate parental mental health difficulties (Health Advisory Service, 1995).

In the UK the incidence of socio-economic disadvantage is said to be higher in minority ethnic populations than in their White counterparts; this view is supported by available statistics (ONS 1998; Smaje 1995). It is also suggested that poverty may interact with ethnicity to impact on the mental health of minority ethnic groups (Beliappa 1991; Cooper *et al.* 1998; Nazaroo 1997).

Indication of socio-economic disadvantage from statistical data

Socio-economic factors encompass a range of areas including housing, employment, income and racism. Available statistics indicate that minority ethnic groups experience significant disadvantage in all of these areas and some minority ethnic groups are at greater risk than others.

Housing

Seventy per cent of all people from minority ethnic groups live in the 88 most deprived local authority districts, compared with 40 per cent of the general population (Social Exclusion Unit 2000).

Some minority ethnic groups are more likely to live in poor housing than others; for example, 40 per cent of Bangladeshi and Pakistani households live in overcrowded housing. Rates of overcrowding for the Irish are twice those of the population as a whole (Social Exclusion Unit 2000), while 20 per cent of the housing occupied by asylum seekers is unfit for human habitation (Garvie 2001).

Employment

Minority ethnic groups account for 7.2 per cent of the working population (ONS 2001).

At 13 per cent, unemployment is more than twice as high among minority ethnic groups compared to their White counterparts at 5.8 per cent (ONS 1998).

As with housing, some minority ethnic groups are at greater risk than others. For example, the rate of unemployment among Pakistani people is 20 per cent, and 23 per cent for Bangladeshi people.

The unemployment rate among young Black (Labour Force Survey category) people aged 16–24 years is 35 per cent compared to 13 per cent among their White counterparts (ONS 1998).

Racism

The risk of being a recipient of racially motivated attacks is said to be greater for minority ethnic groups than for White people. Approximately 4 per cent of Black, 5 per cent of Indian and 8 per cent of Pakistanis experienced racist attacks, compared to 0.5 per cent in the White population (Mirrless-Black *et al.* 1998).

Impact of socio-economic disadvantage on mental health of minority ethnic groups

Studies suggest that material factors (Davey Smith *et al.* 1996; Nazaroo 1997) are relevant to the health of minority ethnic groups and make key contributions to differences in health between minority ethnic groups.

Findings from the Fourth National Survey (Nazaroo 1998) suggest differences in the positions of socio-economic groups that mirror the differences highlighted for health. That is, there were few differences between the Indian and White groups but Pakistanis, Bangladeshis and Caribbeans were worse off in relation to both socio-economic status and health experience. This suggests a strong relationship between class and health.

Limitations of indicators on socio-economic status

There are difficulties in finding indicators of socio-economic status that operate consistently across all ethnic groups, therefore it is necessary to be clear about what is meant by concepts of 'class' and 'material disadvantage'. Based on data from the Fourth National Survey, Nazaroo (1998) highlights that class effects were similar for both minority and majority groups but class did not explain differences between ethnic groups. For example, Pakistanis and Bangladeshis were more likely to report fair or poor health than equivalent Whites within each class group. Interpreting this variation through cultural or genetic factors would be misleading.

A number of other considerations may be relevant such as the variations in income levels that exist among occupations that comprise particular occupational classes (Davey Smith *et al.* 1990). Data from the Fourth National Survey (Nazaroo 1997) illustrates that minority ethnic groups had lower income than White people in the same class; unemployed minority ethnic groups were unemployed for longer than equivalent White people; and some minority ethnic groups had poorer quality housing than Whites regardless of tenure. Other forms of disadvantage that may be relevant but not accounted for by socio-economic indicators include:

- A lifetime perspective whereby the accumulation of disadvantage contributes to differences in health experience. This has particular relevance for migrants who may have experienced a number of life-course transitions and significant deprivation in earlier years. Migration may lead to changes in material resources, social networks and position in the social hierarchy. This requires consideration about how the relationship between lifestyle and health contributes to inequalities.

- Living in a racist society whereby, in addition to experiencing direct (actual) discrimination, knowledge (perceived) about one's relative disadvantage and exclusion may have a significant impact on health (Wilkinson 1996).

- Ecological effects (socio-demographic) – there is some evidence to suggest that environmental factors may have a direct impact on health, over and above individual circumstances (Macintyre *et al.* 1993; Townsend *et al.* 1988). This is of relevance to minority ethnic groups who are concentrated in particular geographical locations that have specific features, different to areas populated by the White majority (Owen 1994).

Recognising both beneficial and harmful effects of lifestyles

It is important to recognise the beneficial as well as harmful aspects in relation to lifestyle (Smaje 1995). For example, concentration of minority ethnic groups in particular locations can be protective of health if this facilitates the development of a community with a strong ethnic identity, which enhances social support and reduces a sense of alienation. Identifying factors that are harmful as well as beneficial, whether in relation to individual beliefs and practices, living environment or other factors, is important to health promotion (Nazaroo 1998).

Socio-economic factors and young people's health

Using data from the British General Household Survey 1991–1994, Cooper *et al.* (1998) looked at whether children and young people's use of health services was related to social class and to their ethnic group. They concluded that:

- There was equitable use of health services in relation to social class. This is different to findings for adults in other studies, suggesting that important differences may exist in the use of health care services by children and young people compared to adults.

- Children and young people living in local authority housing were significantly more likely to use inpatient services. This is said to reflect findings of previous studies that children and young people living in materially deprived conditions are more likely to be admitted to hospital.

- Ethnicity was significantly associated with use in relation to GP, outpatient and inpatient provision. Indian children were more likely to consult a GP than White children. The use of this service by Pakistani and Bangladeshi children was comparable to that by White children. The lowest likelihood of consultation was among Black Caribbean children. Children from all minority groups had a much lower use of outpatient and inpatient services. These differences persisted after controlling for socio-economic and health status.

The overall conclusion of this study suggests that children and young people from minority ethnic groups receive lower rates of referral to secondary care services and poorer health care services than White children and young people.

The impact of racism on mental health

Racism is considered to be one of the factors contributing to mental health difficulties (Clark *et al.* 1999; Fernando 1988; Goldberg and Hodes 1992; MIND 1998). The need to consider actual and perceived aspects of racism is emphasised. One of the consequences of the discrimination faced by minority ethnic groups in employment, housing and education is that it can result in relatively low, or second-rate, access to opportunities. The isolation and distress this can cause is said to be further exacerbated by experiences of discrimination in mental health services. It is suggested that the experience of racism can lead to depression, low self-esteem, anxiety, addiction and a sense of worthlessness. A further consideration relates to dealing with stereotypes; confronted with negative stereotypes, people from minority ethnic groups have a choice of ignoring or confronting them and both options are likely to be stressful.

There are very few studies available that focus on the impact of racism on mental health and even fewer that look at this issue in relation to young people. The two identified here offer some insights on the issues of racism and self-harm and racism and self-belief, in relation to young people.

Goldberg and Hodes (1992) examined the impact of racism on families with adolescent children. Although one limitation of this study is the apparent Eurocentric approach it adopts to family structure and dynamics, it nevertheless highlights a particular approach (the family cycle) to understanding the effect of racism and one of the possible consequences for young people (self-harm). The authors suggest that the emergence of adolescence is said to be associated with major changes in the family:

- For young people adolescence is associated with increasing independence, involvement with peer group and the development of sexual relations.

- Parents may have reached middle age and may be reappraising their own relationships.

- Grandparents may be retiring or showing ill health.

The authors conclude that racist threats and violence can force families to redraw their boundaries in order to protect themselves. Racism may cause parents to become more protective towards their children at a time when young people are striving for increased autonomy and differentiation. It is suggested that this can lead to young people overdosing: 'Racism is an attack on the individual which is reproduced by overdosing as an attack on the self' (Goldberg and Hodes 1992). It should be noted that this study does not comment on the extent to which these changes apply across different cultures.

The importance of addressing both actual and perceived racism in the therapeutic process is described by Bains (2001). The approaches described are based on work undertaken with young people of Indian and Bangladeshi origin who were referred for psychotherapy to a centre in London. Here the focus of the work relates to addressing negative self-belief as a possible outcome of both actual and perceived racism. During the therapeutic process young people were encouraged to:

- understand the psychological effects of racism and how the experience of racism may lead to the development of negative self-belief

- be aware not to internalise negative self-beliefs, to externalise the effects of racism and to perceive specific responses (such as anger, hostility and helplessness) arising from racist experience as functional or appropriate.

The author also states that when dealing with the psychological effects of social processes such as racism, it was extremely difficult to differentiate between whether a response was functional or dysfunctional. Nevertheless, perceived experiences of racism required attention from the therapist in order to engage young people in the therapeutic process.

Victim blaming

Senior and Bhopal (1994) have suggested that the use of ethnic categories alone in epidemiology can result in stereotypical explanations of aetiology that focus on genetic or cultural factors. This in turn leads to victim blaming whereby it is ethnicity itself, rather than the factors associated with it, that are seen as contributing to difficulties (Sheldon and Parker 1992). This is best illustrated by assumptions that 'ethnic' diets can cause health problems. As Pearson (1986) notes, the constraints of poverty on choice of available foods is hardly mentioned – the assumption is that the diets of some minority ethnic groups cause nutritional deficiencies that lead to conditions such as rickets and osteomalacia. Explanations such as this, which focus on culture, can hold individuals responsible for practices and adopt a victim blaming approach.

Conclusions

The different ways of defining ethnicity and the impact this has on research and practice have been outlined in this chapter. Commissioners and providers need to consider the reasons for collecting data on ethnicity, how that data is to be collected (from what source), and how the data can be used to inform the planning and provision of appropriate services.

If one considers the risk factors for experiencing mental illness such as poor education, poor housing, poverty and racism then children from these groups can be considered to be more vulnerable than the White population in the United Kingdom.

References

Atkinson, M., Clark, M., Clay, D., Johnson, M., Owen, D. and Szczepura, A. (2001) *Systematic Review of Ethnicity and Health Service Access for London.* University of Warwick: Centre for Health Services Studies.

Bains, K. (2001) 'Psychotherapy with young people from ethnic minority backgrounds in different community-based settings.' In G. Baruch (ed) *Community Based Psychotherapy With Young People: Evidence and Innovation in Practice.* London: Routledge.

Beliappa, J. (1991) *Illness Or Distress –Alternative Models of Mental Health.* London: Confederation of Indian Organisations (UK).

Bhui, K., Christie, Y. and Bhugra, D. (1995) 'The essential elements of culturally sensitive psychiatric services.' *International Journal of Social Psychiatry 41,* 242–256.

Clark, R., Anderson, N., Clark, V. and Williams, D. R. (1999) 'Racism as a stressor for African Americans.' *American Psychologist 10,* 805–816.

Cooper, H., Smaje, C. and Arber, S. (1998) 'Use of health services by children and young people according to ethnicity and social class: Secondary analysis of a national survey.' *British Medical Journal 317,* 1047–1051.

Davey Smith, G., Bartley, M. and Blane, D. (1990) 'The Black Report on socio-economic inequalities in health 10 years on.' *British Medical Journal 301,* 373–377.

Davey Smith, G., Neaton, J., Wentworth, D., Stamler, J. and Stamler, R. (1996) 'Socioeconomic differentials in mortality risk among screened men screened for the multiple risk factor intervention trial: II. Black Men.' *American Journal of Public Health 86*, 497–504.

Fenton, S. (1999) *Ethnicity: Racism, Class and Culture.* Basingstoke: Macmillan Press.

Fernando, S. (1988) *Race and Culture in Psychiatry.* London: Tavistock/Routledge.

Garvie, D. (2001) *Far from home: the housing of asylum seekers in private rented accommodation.* London: Shelter.

Goldberg, D. and Hodes, M. (1992) 'The poison of racism and the self poisoning of adolescents.' *Journal of Family Therapy 14*, 51–67.

Health Advisory Service (1995) *Child and Adolescent Mental Health Services: Together We Stand.* London: HMSO.

Hodes, M., Creamer, J. and Wolley, J. (1998) 'The cultural meanings of ethnic categories.' *Psychiatric Bulletin 22*, 20–24.

House of Commons Health Committee (1997) *Child and Adolescent Mental Health Services. Health Committee Fourth Report: Session 1996–1997, HC 26-I.* London: HMSO.

Jayarajan, U. (2001) *The Demographic Profile of the Children and Young People Referred to and Seen by Birmingham CAMHS.* Birmingham: Birmingham Children's Hospital NHS Trust.

Kramer, T., Evans, N. and Garralda, M. E. (2000) 'Ethnic diversity among child and adolescent psychiatric attenders.' *Child Psychology and Psychiatry 5*, 169–175.

Kurtz, Z. (1996) *Treating Children Well: A guide to the evidence base in commissioning and managing services for the mental health of children and young people.* London: Mental Health Foundation.

Lakey, J. (1997) *Neighbourhoods and Housing.* London: Policy Studies Institute.

Leech, K. (1989) *A Question in Dispute: The Debate about an 'Ethnic' Question in the Census.* London: Runnymede Trust.

Lloyd, K. (1998) 'Ethnicity, social inequality and mental illness.' *British Medical Journal 316*, 1763–1770.

Macintyre, S., Maciver, S. and Soomans, A. (1993) 'Area, Class and Health: Should we be focusing on places or people?' *Journal of Social Policy 22*, 213–214.

Messent, P. and Murrell, M. 'Research leading to action: A study of accessibility of a CAMH service to ethnic minority families.' *Child and Adolescent Mental Health 8*, 3, 118–124.

MIND (1998) *Factsheets – The Mental Health of the African and Caribbean Community in Britain.* London: MIND Publications.

Minnis, H., Kelly, E., Bradby, H., Oglethorpe, R., Raine, W., Cockburn, D. (2003) 'Cultural and Language Mismatch: Clinical Complications.' *Clinical Child and Psychology and Psychiatry 8*, 2, 1791–1186.

Mirrless-Black, C., Budd, T., Partridge, S. and Mayhew, P. (1998) *The 1998 British Crime Survey: England and Wales.* London: Home Office.

Nazaroo, J. (1997) *The Health of Britain's Ethnic Minorities: Findings from a National Survey.* London: Policy Studies Institute.

Nazaroo, J. (1998) 'Genetic, cultural or socio-economic vulnerability? Explaining ethnic inequalities in health.' *Sociology of Health and Illness 20*, 710–730.

Office for National Statistics (1998) *Labour Force Survey*. London: HMSO.

Office for National Statistics (2001) *Population Trends (No. 105)*. London: HMSO.

Owen, D. (1994) 'Spatial variations in ethnic minority group populations in Great Britain.' *Population Trends (No.78)*. London: HMSO.

Owen, D. (1996) 'Size, structure and growth of the ethnic minority populations.' In D. Coleman and J. Salt (eds) *Ethnicity in the 1991 Census* Volume 1. London: HMSO.

Pearson, M. (1986) 'The politics of ethnic minority health studies.' In T. Rathwell and D. Phillips (eds) *Health, Race and Ethnicity* London: Croom Helm.

Ratcliffe, P. (1999) 'Housing inequality and "race": some critical reflections on the concept of "social exclusion".' *Ethnic and Racial Studies 22*, 1–22.

Raleigh, S. V. and Balarajan, R. (1994) 'Public Health and the 1991 Census.' *British Medical Journal 309*, 287–288.

Schuman, J. (1999) 'The ethnic minority populations of Great Britain – latest estimates.' *Population Trends (No. 96)*. London: HMSO.

Senior, P. A. and Bhopal, R. (1994) 'Ethnicity as a variable in epidemiological research.' *British Medical Journal 309*, 327–330.

Sheldon, T. and Parker, H. (1992) 'Race and Ethnicity in Health Research.' *Journal of Public Health Medicine 14*, 104–110.

Smaje, C. (1995) *Health, race and ethnicity: Making sense of the evidence*. London: Kings Fund Institute.

Social Exclusion Unit (2000) *Minority Ethnic Issues in Social Exclusion and Neighbourhood Renewal*. London: Cabinet Office.

Townsend, P., Phillimore, P. and Beattie, A. (1988) *Health and Deprivation: Inequality and the North*. London: Routledge.

Williams, D., Lavizzo-Mourey, R. and Warren, R. (1994) 'The concept of race and health status in America.' *Public Health Reports (No. 109)*. Oxford: Oxford University Press.

Wilkinson, R. (1996) *Unhealthy Societies: Afflictions of Inequality*. London: Routledge.

2 The Cultural Relevance of the Mental Health Disciplines

Begum Maitra

Western ethnopsychology

The record of how psychology and psychiatry have dealt with the subject of 'racial' difference is, not unexpectedly, marked by the history of relationships between the West and the non-West (e.g. colonialism, slavery, large-scale migrations – see Littlewood and Lipsedge 1989). Noting the curious disinterest within psychiatry/psychology towards cultural differences, Shweder, a key figure in cultural psychology, suggests that the Platonic idea of 'an inherent (fixed, universal) and central (transcendent, abstract) processing mechanism, a psychic unity to humankind, will never be seriously threatened by the mere existence of performance differences between individuals or populations' (1991, p. 79).

The historical influences that have shaped Western psychology and its allied disciplines, have been dealt with by several writers (Doi 1990; Littlewood 2000; Skultans 2000; Squire 2000; van Langenhove 1995). That these disciplines are 'ethnocentric' is scarcely surprising (what else could they be?), since any theory of mind, and its disorders, arises out of local cultural constructions of normality, deviance and interpersonal relationships; 'ethnotheories' are the rationale for why cultural practices 'work'. The dominant culture/discourse seldom needs to speak its name, being defined in contrast to the more explicit naming of marginal and subordinated subjects (Griffin 2000). Early cross-cultural research and writings focused on the comparative epidemiology of major mental illnesses, that is, forms identified in the West and believed to be universal. Unusual presentations not found in the West – the so-called 'culture-bound syndromes' (Yap 1951) – were initially thought to represent local versions of universal cultural disorders. In current thinking these have come to signify distinctive and consistent patterns of behaviour, closely related to the culture's understanding of self and normative experience, which may or may not be considered pathological (i.e. evidence of illness) in the terminology of Western psychiatry. According to some, these 'stylised expressive traditional behaviours' are expressions of fairly common personal conflict in forms that are culturally condoned contraventions of the norm.[1]

Subsequent research into race/culture has become bogged down in methodological questions of comparable concepts and language, the universal validity of Western diagnostic/screening instruments and the value of attempts at cross-cultural validation. While these are by no means unimportant issues, epidemiological method provides little understanding of how cultures work, or of the complexity of changing relationships between ethnicity, identity, belief and practice. In sharing the basic universalistic claims of general psychology, comparative or cross-cultural psychology aims at little more than finding culture-fair tests that will, hopefully, eliminate the 'noise' of culture to reveal the universal central mechanism.

Child psychiatry had, until quite recently, followed suit to focus on comparative rates of disorder (e.g. Rutter et al. 1974, 1975), and allied issues, such as service utilisation (i.e. clinic attendance and drop-out rates). Explanations offered for differences in rates of disorder[2] appear to work on the expectation of equal rates universally, and cite 'culture' in usually simple, 'linear' fashion. For higher rates in minority ethnic groups explanations commonly rely on social disadvantage (socio-economic, or rooted in racial discrimination) or disadvantage arising out of cultural practices/difference (as in high rates of Asian adolescent self-harm); where rates are lower, this may be attributed to the ethnic community's reluctance to seek help (due to culturally based ignorance, stigma, rejection of services that are culturally insensitive/irrelevant), selection bias in referral or cultural protective factors. Cultural information, when presented, is often fragmentary, drawn from diverse cultural groups loosely gathered into spurious 'ethnic' categories (e.g. 'Asians'), and inadequately contextualised. Such information is difficult to use in clinical work, and rarely addresses the vital issue of the theoretical inadequacies of basic professional trainings. Bose (2003) summarises some of the central issues, such as problems of methodology, diagnostic difficulties, and the relationship between cultural expectations and patterns of disorder in children.

More recently, a slowly growing body of writing by bicultural clinicians (Bose 1997; Dwivedi 1995; Lau 1994; Maitra 1995; Malik 2000; Timimi 1995) indicates a concern to provide culturally detailed, 'thick'[3] descriptions (Krause 1998) that address the gap between cross-cultural (quantitative) data and ethnographic accounts of children (usually of a non-clinical sort). The recent surge of attention to ethical practice, across differences of gender and sexuality as well as culture, has produced a wealth of publications (e.g. Gorell Barnes 1998; Maitra and Miller 1995; Patel 2000), including guidelines for training (Miller and Thomas 1994; Moodley 2002). However, the theoretical and practice skills that the qualifying professional is rated on continues to be dominated by Western models of the 'mental' functions, and 'culture' remains largely peripheral to the training of child mental health clinicians (Maitra 2003). Despite the welcome inclusion of culture in recent influential texts (e.g. Rutter and Nikapota 2002), the limited space allocated to it highlights the continuing assumption that the themes familiar to Western psychology (and middle-class professional culture) are of universal importance and validity.

While anthropology has a long tradition of cultural studies of childhood, there is still a strong tendency to see patterns found in mainstream European-American society as the norm.

> The ever-vigilant parents who never miss a chance to create an instructional moment for their child are now taken as the norm, and descriptions of these parents in action have become a staple of the research literature in child development. (Lancy 1996, p. 16)

Alternative patterns are seen as aberrant and as requiring some explanation.

Contemporary trends in child mental health practice, namely in the influence of multidisciplinary teams and of the psychotherapies[4] (and systemic thinking in particular), show a reduced emphasis on biomedical paradigms. The daily practice of most child mental health clinicians in Britain, whether or not they work with multicultural populations, reflects a greater awareness of subjective bias (based on profession, class or culture) and a willingness to abandon the traditional search for 'objective' facts in favour of a co-construction of meanings (both about problems and solutions).[5] Therapy may focus less often on the individual child than on the child, within its family and other significant relationships.

Considering the universal dependency of children on carers (whatever the structure of local child care strategy), it is striking that this 'psychosocial' model of the child is so rarely visible in other professional contexts that consider children, such as in child protection (Maitra 1996) or child health and welfare. Speaking of the international children's rights movement, Burman (1996) notes the tendency to portray the 'social' only in terms of the 'interpersonal', giving rise to what she calls a 'desert island model of mother and child', suspended from broader social relations.

The scope of this chapter does not permit detailed discussion of the contributions of research in cultural psychology. It will therefore focus on some of the central assumptions of Western child psychology, and point to studies that frame the diversity of beliefs and practices in interlocking systems of cultural belief and meaning. Hopefully, this will encourage clinicians to explore the mesh of changing belief and practice among the cultural groups, both indigenous and immigrant, that they work with. Furthermore, awareness of the cultural specificity of what has traditionally been considered universal by Western professionals, and unquestioningly applied to all cultures, will lead to a wider, more inclusive view of children's lives and relationships.

Cultural psychology

Considering the long tradition in anthropology of studying how cultures influence those very same areas central to mental health (e.g. language, emotion, personality, motivation and so on), it is curious that academic child psychiatry and psychology have had so little exchange with the field of cultural psychology.[6] Indeed, as shown above, there is a greater affinity between the orientation of contemporary child mental health practice and that of the fieldwork of cultural anthropologists, than with biomedical psychiatry. The field of cultural psychology is not limited to a study of non-Western 'traditional' cultures; it is essentially interdisciplinary, engaging with debates in anthropology, philosophy, cultural studies, education, sociology, literary studies and linguistics. Debates about language and meaning (treated as a profoundly social construction dependent on the specific context rather than a true reflection of 'facts') are central to this enterprise. Cultural psychology, Shweder writes, is:

> the study of the ways subject and object, self and other, psyche and culture, person and context, figure and ground, practitioner and practice, live together, require each other, and dynamically, dialectically, and jointly make each other up. (1991, p. 73)

In contrast to the traditional Western view of the individual as independent of and acting upon their environment, he points out that the basic idea of cultural psychology is that every human being's subjectivity and mental life are altered through the process of seizing meanings and resources from some sociocultural environment and using them.

> A sociocultural environment is an *intentional* world. It is an intentional world because its existence is real, factual, and forceful, but only so long as there exists a community of persons whose beliefs, desires, emotions, purposes, and other mental representations are directed at, and thereby influenced by, it. (Shweder 1991, p.74, my emphasis)

Some messages from cultural research

Why parents have children

The low birth rates and voluntary limitation of family size common in parts of Europe and North America are unusual in much of the rest of the world. Research from many parts of Africa and South Asia repeatedly show high fertility, and with women choosing to have large numbers of children for a great variety of reasons. Why do parents have children, and how does this motivation determine how much, or in what way, parents invest in children? Lancy (1996) suggests the biological imperative imputed to all animals – that of ensuring that one's genes are passed along. He proposes that Western societies lie at the 'child-centered' end of a continuum, while admitting that parental anxiety about maximising the opportunities for development of small numbers of offspring is not common among all classes of these societies, but located more in the middle classes. Other writers (e.g. Berger 1993; Davies 1993) describe different relationships between socio-economic structures and the value accorded to children in contemporary Western families. Lancy (1996) also suggests that agrarian societies see children primarily as economic assets; their optimal parenting strategy lies in high fertility, reflecting the high infant/child mortality, the high value of unskilled child labour, the low cost of child-rearing, and numerous children who will provide support in the parents' later years. Yang, Thornton and Fricke (2000) refers to motivations related to other considerations (specifically, to Tai-wanese ancestor-worship), and to complex traditions that had, until recently,[7] emphasised the essential requirement for male offspring to continue the descent line. Women's labour, education, social investment in daughters and other complex gender-related variables are equally important in how groups organise child care (Kutty 1989; Levine et al. 1996; MacCormack 1988; Pelto 1987; Zeitlin 1996).

Child-care, parenting values and routines

Children are shaped within the metaphorical space of a 'developmental niche' (Super and Harkness 1986) that includes the physical and social settings the child is exposed to, prevailing child-rearing strategies and folk theories about how children develop. In a study of child-rearing values in the Republic of Belarus (after the collapse of the Soviet Union), the three most important qualities in children identified by adult respondents were 'feeling of responsibility', 'hard work', and 'tolerance and respect for other people' (Vardomatskii and Pankhurst 2000). However, the teaching of these qualities may not be seen as a task for parents. In a sample of more than a hundred societies, Weisner and Gallimore (1977) found that 40 per cent of infants and 80 per cent of toddlers are cared for primarily by someone other than the mother. In a detailed study of Gusii child care practices, Levine et al. (1996) describe the care of infants between the ages of 6 and 18 months by omoreri, older child-carers aged between 6 and 9 years. This may appear startling to Western professionals who have grown accustomed to thinking of care by children as equivalent to (parental) neglect or abuse.

While verbal stimulation of infants and young children by adults to encourage language acquisition[8] may be common among Western mothers, its appearance in Western child mental health texts (e.g. Graham 1991) rarely mentions the cultural and class specificity of this practice. Lancy (1996) notes that it is not the norm among mothers outside the American mainstream or in several other cultures (Ochs and Schieffelin 1984). Anthropological studies suggest that 'proto-conversation' between mother and infant is not a universal cultural script; it is not seen as a useful source of information, socialisation or emotional exchange, and may be expressly avoided. Culture-specific norms might exempt babies from verbal interaction altogether, or direct the mother to attend to crying and ignore babbling, and prescribe formulaic routines such as lullabies that are not overtly designed to stimulate communication. In a comparative study of rural Kenyan, Mexican and middle-class American mothers, Richman, Miller and LeVine (1992) found intracultural variation in maternal response to babies that was associated with years of schooling. They explained this, not as evidence of 'knowledge' about child stimulation, but as an effect of participation in institutionalised systems of communication.

Other child-parent exchanges (such as eye-contact and praise among Gusii children) may be discouraged since these would foster attitudes incongruent with acceptable codes of hierarchical behaviour in adult society. In exploring literature from many cultures, Lancy (1996) found only one area in which nearly all parents seemed to take on the didactic role of teacher – namely in teaching manners, polite speech formulas, and respect for the child's age and class superiors. Where formal education is not compulsory children usually play in mixed age groups, learning from and supervised by older children. Play then acts as a vehicle for learning, through imitation of adult activity at increasing levels of skill, and may be promoted by adults who focus more on 'concrete' imitation of adult skills, rather than on the 'symbolic' or pleasurable aspects of the child's play.

Each cultural group's schema for child rearing contains a 'calendar' of developmental milestones. A survey of 50 societies found two ages when adult expectations of children change: at five to seven years, when children are widely believed to have developed 'sense', and at the onset of puberty (Rogoff 1975). These benchmarks, often accompanied by rites of passage, define the child's reference group and act as an incentive for behaving in age-appropriate ways.

Culture and the self

The Western folk model of the self that underlies psychological theory (as it does psychoanalysis) conceives of the adult person capable of agency and intention as separate from others, with the body as the source of his (more often than 'her') identity, and within which experience is located. That these are not universally held beliefs is now amply documented in anthropological accounts of other cultures – the self being less distinctly separate from others (human/animal/spirit, kin/non-kin); the body less clearly marked from mind and mental functions, from spirit and so on (Kakar 1990; Moore 1994; Morris 1994). This variety in concepts of the person, and how the self or selves are thought about is closely linked with adult views of the nature of children (e.g. Fruzetti, Ostor and Barnett 1992), and to parental attitudes towards individual children (such as in naming practices, attitudes to child death and 'replacement' children, the significance of sibling order, and so on – see also Maitra 1995). It is important to remember that to informants from within the culture these beliefs may seem so 'natural' as to be unremarkable, and not easily available for discussion.

Emotion and attachment

To those who are concerned about uncontrolled cultural relativism, and the importance of establishing what is universal, 'attachment' forms something of a rallying cry. Rutter and Nikapota write:

> There is every reason to suppose that the development of selective social attachments is culture-universal (...) as a biological phenomenon that stems from humans being social animals. (2002, p.279)

While the fact that children develop selective attachments may seem self-evident, the nature of these emotional bonds, their behavioural expression, stability and consequences remain open to cultural influences.

Several researchers have suggested that although the repertoire of infant attachment behaviours may be universal, the selection, shaping and interpretation of these appear to be culturally patterned (e.g. van Ijzendoorn 1990). Harwood, Miller and Irizarry (1995) provide a useful summary of attachment and cross-cultural research, and describe a comparative study of Puerto Rican and American mothers and their children. They found that maternal preference (determined by culture and social class) predicted child behaviour, both in general and in situations such as Ainsworth's Strange Situation (Ainsworth and Wittig 1969). Behaviours rated as indicating insecure attachments in American children were encouraged by Puerto Rican mothers, as evidence of obedient, well-mannered and properly socialised children. Such findings suggest caution when basing judgements of poor parenting, and predicting emotional consequences, on ratings of attachment behaviour across cultures.

Children at work

James, Jenks and Prout (1998) discuss the longstanding acknowledgement of children's work in societies outside the industrialised 'North', recognising its variety and also the complexity of its meanings for the child. Within industrialised societies 'protectionist' discourses, premised on children's vulnerability and need for protection, reflect the shift of demand away from unskilled towards more skilled and educated labour and the relocation of children in compulsory education. These discourses distinguish between 'child work', which does not detract from the allegedly 'essential' activities of children (namely leisure, play and education), and 'child labour', which impairs the health and development of children. While some work raises health and safety concerns, little attention is given to children's own accounts of benefits and losses – of paid employment outside the home, against unpaid forms of work within the home (e.g. farming, caring) and unpaid school work.[9] Detailed local studies are necessary of the circumstances of working children since the content and meaning of work is highly dependent on its social, cultural and economic context.

Child rights

Tracing the development of the current position of the child in Britain, Davies (1993) refers to changing trends in marriage customs and the law. Children are no longer the highest priority in the contract of marriage, and are now seen as possessing a 'natural' individuality from birth, 'which gradually but inevitably, and as of right, lays claim to an autonomy exercisable irrespective of parental views or wishes...' (p.91). These 'natural' rights are not circumscribed by a sense of 'natural obligations' towards parents or towards siblings.

Burman (1996) draws attention to the fact that international legislation on children's rights, based on a Western philosophy of liberal individualism, invokes and maintains Western definitions of psychological development (and associated 'needs') as though these were universally valid. Despite the moral power associated with this language of universal rights and needs, such concepts fit uneasily within other cultural contexts, failing especially to address the complexity of relations between women and children. This is particularly relevant in therapy with immigrant families when the consideration of their children's needs and rights may need to be framed within the family's needs for survival (as a unit, or multiple interlinking units, in economic, cultural, even hierarchical forms), and only gradually shaped, if relevant, to reflect indigenous British expectations.

Ethnicity and identity

Ethnicity and identity are sometimes thought about as inextricably linked, but more so for minority groups than the dominant White group, however varied their ethnic origins might be. While a wish to define the ethnicity of minority groups may sometimes be framed as a positive step intended, say, to monitor equity of service provision, it creates categories[10] that have little resonance with cultural identity, and spuriously privilege one criterion of difference over others (Singh 1997). A collapsing of ethnic and national identities (e.g. 'White' British, 'Indian' British) potentially problematises ethnicity and seeps into discourses on cultural difference.

Cornell and Hartmann (1998) enlarge the focus to consider the large variety of group factors that influence the construction of ethnic identities within wider society. In a fascinating exploration of ethnic identities within American society, and drawing on studies from around the world, they discuss the impact of factors such as the size, distribution and political clout of a group that may determine its representation of itself as an 'ethnic community'. Intra-group differences such as the sex ratios of migrant populations (formed by immigration patterns and related laws in the host country) and cultural prohibitions within the migrant and host groups (such as against inter-ethnic sexual relations/marriage) influence the size and homogeneity of the evolving group. Subtle and complex psychological factors interact with apparently 'objective' descriptors of the group, such as the social class and education of immigrants, to contribute to a sense of security and confidence - to what has been termed 'institutional completeness', indicating the capacity of the community to satisfy the needs of its members. Adult immigrant confidence greatly influences the reality of their children's lives, and may be more significant in the child's sense of self, identity/ies and self-esteem than simpler discourses around experiences of racism.

Culture, cognition and psychometry

Ethnographic studies have shown that minority children come to school with distinct styles of cognition (Cohen 1969), learning (Phillips 1976), communication (Gumperz 1981) and interaction. That these should lead to teaching and learning difficulties and to problems with the emotional adjustment of school-going minority children is thus not surprising. Looking at the academic performance of minority ethnic students in the United States, Ogbu (1990) discusses a number of ways in which ethnic group (immigrants and involuntary minorities - that is Black and Mexican Americans, and American Indians) differences affect attitudes to literacy. Historical and wider societal forces encourage or discourage literacy, and these attitudes may be mediated collectively, through people's interpretations of their social reality and the place of literacy in that reality. Ogbu describes the contrasting historical experiences of immigrants and involuntary minorities that result in contrasting cultural models and social identities; cultural models conducive to academic striving and success result in greater academic success among immigrant minority groups.

Other reasons for why minority children from different ethnic groups might show different levels of performance lie in the school or classroom environment, both in the quality of relationships and in culturally shaped beliefs about learning. In a comparative study of how mathematics is taught in elementary school classrooms in China, Japan and the United States, Stigler and Perry (1990) show how cultural beliefs about the nature of individual differences (American belief in innate abilities and unique limitations), classroom organisation (whether to provide indi-vidualised learning or uniform educational experiences), and cultural attitudes towards public evaluation of performances (American beliefs that it would be cruel to discuss errors publicly, especially since mathe-matical ability is seen as innate and no fault of the student's) result in far greater learning among students in the first two countries than in the United States.

The power relationships between medicine and neuropsychology may have led in the past to the use of psychometry to support racist ideology (Murphy 2000). Many limitations persist, such as the cultural bias of tests and the materials used, the difficulty with finding equivalent words/constructs in other cultures/languages, and uncertainties about whether re-standardisation has been undertaken for other cultures. Murphy lists supplementary information that may assist in obtaining a truer picture of the subject's abilities – alertness to the interviewer's cultural background, a thorough history of the client's background, the use of cultural informants, the use of non-verbally mediated assessment, attention to the choice of tests for those whose mother tongue is not English and greater care in interpreting these results.

Conclusion

It is hoped that this brief account of cultural studies from around the world shows the richness of data already available about the diversity of children's lives, and that children reach developmental goals, defined by their cultural group, through a wide variety of routes. While simple corre-lations may not be made between what the literature may say about another culture's modes of function and the child and family in the Western clinic, a wider reading will allow the clinician more room to plan therapeutic strategy and goals that are not overly determined by the cultural assumptions embedded within the Western mental health disciplines.

References

Ainsworth, M.D.S. and Wittig, B.A. (1969) 'Attachment and exploratory behaviour of one-year olds in a strange situation.' In B.M. Foss (ed) *Determinants of Infant Behaviour.* London: Methuen.

Berger, B. (1993) 'The bourgeois family and modern society.' In J. Davies, B. Berger and A. Carlson (eds) *The Family: Is it just another lifestyle choice?* London: IEA Health and Welfare Unit.

Bose, R. (1997) 'Psychiatry and the popular conception of possession among the Bangladeshis in London.' *International Journal of Social Psychiatry 43*, 1–15.

Bose, R. (2003) 'Child Psychiatry in a Multicultural Context.' In D. Skuse (ed) *Child Psychology and Psychiatry.* Oxford: The Medicine Publishing Co. Ltd.

Burman, E. (1996) 'Local, Global or Globalized? Child development and international child rights legislation.' *Childhood 3*, 45–66.

Cohen, R.A. (1969) 'Conceptual styles, culture conflict, and non-verbal test of intelligence.' *American Anthropologist 71*, 828–856.

Cornell, S. and Hartmann, D. (1998) *Ethnicity and Race: Making identities in a changing world.* Thousand Oaks, California: Pine Forge Press.

Davies, J. (1993) 'From household to family to individualism.' In J. Davies, B. Berger and A. Carlson (eds) *The Family: Is it just another lifestyle choice?* London: IEA Health and Welfare Unit.

Doi, T. (1990) 'The Cultural Assumptions of Psychoanalysis.' In J.W. Stigler, R.A. Shweder and G. Herdt (eds) *Cultural Psychology: Essays on comparative human development.* Cambridge: Cambridge University Press.

Dwivedi, K.N. (1995) 'Culture and Personality.' In K.N. Dwivedi and V.P. Varma (eds) *Meeting the Needs of Ethnic Minority Children – A handbook for professionals.* London: Jessica Kingsley Publishers.

Fruzetti, L., Ostor, A. and Barnett, S. (1992) 'The cultural construction of the person in Bengal and Tamilnadu.' In A. Ostor, L. Fruzetti and S. Barnett (eds) *Concepts of Person: Kinship, Caste and Marriage in India.* New Delhi: Oxford University Press.

Goodnow, J.J. (1990) 'The socialization of cognition: what's involved?' In J.W. Stigler, R.A. Shweder and G. Herdt (eds) *Cultural Psychology: Essays on comparative human development.* Cambridge: Cambridge University Press.

Gorell Barnes, G. (1998) *Family Therapy in Changing Times.* London: Macmillan.

Graham, P. (1991) *Child Psychiatry: A developmental approach.* Oxford: Oxford Medical Publications.

Griffin, C. (2000) 'More than simply talk and text: Psychologists as cultural ethnographers.' In C. Squire (ed) *Culture in Psychology.* London: Routledge.

Gumperz, J.J. (1981) 'Conversational inferences and classroom learning.' In J. Green and C. Wallatt (eds) *Ethnographic Approaches to Face-to-Face Interaction.* Norwood, NJ: Ablex.

Harwood, R.L., Miller, J.G. and Irizarry, N.L. (1995) *Culture and Attachment: Perceptions of the Child in Context.* London: Guilford Press.

Heald, S. and Deluz, A. (eds) (1994) *Anthropology and Psychoanalysis: An encounter through culture.* London: Routledge.

James, A., Jenks, C. and Prout, A. (1998) *Theorizing Childhood.* Cambridge: Polity Press.

Kakar, S. (1990) 'Stories from Indian Psychoanalysis: context and text.' In J.W. Stigler, R.A. Shweder and G. Herdt (eds)) *Cultural Psychology: Essays on comparative human development.* Cambridge: Cambridge University Press.

Krause, I.-B. (1998) *Therapy across Culture.* London: Sage.

Kutty, V.R. (1989) 'Women's Education and its Influence on Attitudes to Aspects of Child-Care in a Village Community in Kerala.' *Social Science and Medicine 29,* 11, 1299–1303.

Lancy, D.F. (1996) *Playing on the Mother-Ground: Cultural routines for children's development.* New York: Guilford Press.

Lau, A. (1994) 'Gender, Culture and Family Life.' *Context 20,* 13–16.

Levine, R.A., Dixon, S., Levine, S., Dixon, S., Richman, A., Herbert, Leiderman, P. and Keefer, C. (1996) *Child Care and Culture: Lessons from Africa.* Cambridge: Cambridge University Press.

Littlewood, R. (2000) 'Psychiatry's Culture.' In V. Skultans and J. Cox (eds) *Anthropological Approaches to Psychological Medicine: Crossing bridges.* London: Jessica Kingsley Publishers.

Littlewood, R. and Lipsedge, M. (1989) *Aliens and Alienists: Ethnic minorities and psychiatry.* 2nd Edition. London: Unwin Hyman.

MacCormack, C.P. (1988) 'Health and the social power of women.' *Social Science and Medicine 26,* 7, 677–683.

Maitra, B. (1995) 'Giving due consideration to families' racial and cultural backgrounds.' In P. Reder and C. Lucey (eds) *Assessment of Parenting: Psychiatric and Psychological Considerations.* London: Routledge.

Maitra, B. (1996) 'Child abuse: A universal "diagnostic" category? The implication of culture in definition and assessment.' *International Journal of Social Psychiatry 42,* 4, 287–304.

Maitra, B. (2003) 'Would cultural matching ensure culturally competent assessments?' In P. Reder, S. Duncan and C. Lucey (eds) *Studies in the Assessment of Parenting.* London: Routledge.

Maitra, B. and Miller, A. (1995) 'Children, families and therapists: clinical considerations and ethnic minority cultures.' In K.N. Dwivedi and V.P. Varma (eds) *Meeting the Needs of Ethnic Minority Children – A handbook for professionals.* London: Jessica Kingsley Publishers.

Malik, R. (2000) 'Culture and emotions: depression among Pakistanis.' In C. Squire (ed) *Culture in Psychology* London: Routledge.

Miller, A. and Thomas, L. (1994) 'Introducing ideas about racism and culture into family therapy training'. *Context 20*, Autumn (Canterbury: AFT Publishing).

Moodley, P. (2002) 'Building a culturally capable workforce – an educational approach to delivering equitable mental health services.' *Psychiatric Bulletin 26*, 63–65.

Moore, H. (1994) 'Gendered Persons: dialogues between anthropology and psychoanalysis.' In S. Heald and A. Deluz (eds) *Anthropology and Psychoanalysis: An encounter through culture*. London: Routledge.

Morris, B. (1994) *Anthropology of the Self: The individual in cultural perspective.* London: Pluto Press.

Murphy, L. (2000) 'Neuropsychology'. In N. Patel (ed) *Clinical Psychology, 'Race' and Culture: A training manual.* London: BPS.

Ochs, E. and Schieffelin, B.B. (1984) 'Language acquisition and socialization: Three developmental stories and their implications.' In R. Shweder and R.L. Levine (eds) *Culture Theory: Essays on mind, self and society.* New York: Cambridge University Press.

Ogbu, J.U. (1990) 'Cultural mode, identity, and literacy.' In J.W. Stigler, R.A. Shweder and G. Herdt (eds) *Cultural Psychology: Essays on Comparative Human Development.* Cambridge: Cambridge University Press.

Patel, N. (ed) (2000) *Clinical Psychology, 'Race' and Culture: A Training Manual.* London: BPS Books.

Pelto, G.H. (1987) 'Cultural Issues in Maternal and Child Health and Nutrition.' *Social Science and Medicine 25*, 6, 553–559.

Phillips, S.U. (1976) 'Commentary: Access to power and maintenance of ethnic identity as goals of multicultural education.' *Anthropology and Education Quarterly 7*, 30–32.

Richman, A.L., Miller, P.M. and Levine, R.A. (1992) 'Cultural and Educational Variations in Maternal Responsiveness.' *Developmental Psychology 28*, 4, 614–621.

Rogoff, B. (1975) 'Age of assignment of roles and responsibilities to children.' *Human Development 18*, 353–369.

Rutter, M., Yule, W., Berger, M., Yule, B., Morton, J. and Bagley, C. (1974) 'Children of West Indian immigrants. I. Rates of behavioural deviance and of psychiatric disorder.' *Journal of Child Psychology and Psychiatry 15*, 241–262.

Rutter, M., Yule, B., Morton, J. and Bagley, C. (1975) 'Children of West Indian immigrants. III. Home circumstances and family patterns.' *Journal of Child Psychology and Psychiatry 16*, 105–123.

Rutter, M. and Nikapota, A. (2002) 'Culture, Ethnicity, Society and Psychopathology.' In M. Rutter and E. Taylor (eds) *Child and Adolescent Psychiatry.* 4th Edition. Oxford: Blackwell Science.

Shweder, R. A. (1991) 'Cultural Psychology: What Is It?' In *Thinking through Cultures: Expeditions in Cultural Psychology.* Cambridge, MA: Harvard University Press.

Singh, S.P. (1997) 'Editorial: Ethnicity in psychiatric epidemiology: need for precision.' *British Journal of Psychiatry 171*, 305–308.

Skultans, V. (2000) 'Remembering and Forgetting: Anthropology and Psychiatry: The changing relationship.' In V. Skultans and J. Cox (eds) *Anthropological Approaches to Psychological Medicine: Crossing bridges.* London: Jessica Kingsley Publishers.

Squire, C. (ed) (2000) *Culture in Psychology.* London: Routledge.

Stigler, J.W. and Perry, M. (1990) 'Mathematics learning in Japanese, Chinese, and American classrooms.' In J.W. Stigler, R.A. Shweder and G. Herdt (eds) *Cultural Psychology: Essays on Comparative Human Development.* Cambridge: Cambridge University Press.

Super, C.M. and Harkness, S. (1986) 'The developmental niche: A conceptualisation at the interface of child and culture.' *International Journal of Behavioural Development 9*, 545–569.

Timimi, S. (1995) 'Adolescence in Immigrant Arab Families.' *Psychotherapy 32*, 141–149.

van Ijzendoorn, M.H. (1990) (ed) 'Cross-cultural validity of attachment theory – Special Issue.' *Human Development 33.*

van Langenhove, L. (1995) 'The Theoretical Foundations of Experimental Psychology and its Alternatives.' In J.A. Smith, R. Harre and L. van Langenhove (eds) *Rethinking Psychology.* London: Sage.

Vardomatskii, A. and Pankhurst, J.G. (2000) 'Belarus on the cusp of change: The relationship between religion and family in a newly open religious market.' In S.K. Houseknecht and J.G. Pankhurst (eds) *Family, Religion, Social Change in Diverse Societies.* Oxford: Oxford University Press.

Weisner, T. and Gallimore, R. (1977) 'My brother's keeper.' *Current Anthropology 18* (2), 169–180.

Yang, L., Thornton, A. and Fricke, T. (2000) 'Religion and family formation in Taiwan: The decline of ancestral authority.' In S.K. Houseknecht and J.G. Pankhurst (eds) *Family, Religion, Social Change in Diverse Societies.* Oxford: Oxford University Press.

Yap, P.M. (1951) 'Mental diseases peculiar to certain cultures.' *Journal of Mental Science 97*, 313–337.

Zeitlin, M. (1996) 'My child is my crown: Yoruba parental theories and practices in early childhood.' In S. Harkness and C.M. Super (eds) *Parents' Cultural Belief Systems: Their origins, expressions, and consequences.* London: Guilford Press.

Notes

1   Thus anorexia nervosa, dissociative identity disorder and chronic fatigue syndrome are forms that arise within Western industrialised nations (Rutter and Nikapota 2002).

2   It is important to bear in mind that these are Western categories of disorder.

3   Descriptions of action/event in terms of its meaning, and of all possible meanings that could be given to it, in the context in which it took place.

4   Whatever the direction of influence, it is very common for psychologists and psychiatrists working with children to have additional formal trainings in at least one of the family, group or individual psychotherapies.

5   These trends reflect the contemporary shift away from the older dominant cultural belief (in objective science) to a post-modern acceptance of multiple coexisting truths, itself a consequence of the fluidity of global movements, family and society common to multicultural urban settings.

6   Heald and Deluz (1994) comment on the fluctuating relationship between anthropology and psychoanalysis. Skultans (2000) acknowledges the role of critical self-knowledge in anthropological fieldwork, the subjective dimension of observation having won respectability over earlier claims to a properly scientific objectivity.

7   Successive cohorts of Taiwanese have shown a decline in the numbers who rated 'maintaining the family chain' highly as a life value.

8   Lancy (1996) describes the characteristics of 'motherese' among the American middle-class mothers – the infant is placed *en face*, with the use of a baby-talk register, a special lexicon and higher pitch.

9   The authors discuss the intriguing suggestion that children are part of societal division of labour by means of their work in school, producing themselves as an embodied form of societal investment and contributing to the national economy later through employment.

10   For example, the Office of Population Census categories of 'Indian', 'Pakistani', 'Bangladeshi' reflect fairly recent national boundaries, not cultural or 'ethnic' difference. What is more problematic is the way in which these categories appear to normalise a series of regional conflicts that arose as a consequence of British colonial activities.

3 The Epidemiology of Mental Health Problems in Children and Adolescents from Minority Ethnic Groups in the UK

Paul Ramchandani

The purpose of this chapter is to examine the contribution that epidemiological studies have made, and could make, to our understanding of the mental health problems faced by children and adolescents from minority ethnic groups in the United Kingdom. This chapter is in two main parts. The first looks at the place of epidemiological studies in cross-cultural research and highlights some of the potential pitfalls in such research. It ends with a suggested checklist, which readers may (or may not) wish to use when appraising such studies. The second part summarises the principal epidemiological studies that have been published to date (2002). Finally a list of other resources, in the form of a reference list, has been provided.

It is important to emphasise from the start that there are a number of limits placed on the scope of this chapter. Firstly, it is examining the mental health needs of children and adolescents only – not those of adults (although the needs of the two groups are often interlinked), and not the other medical, social and educational needs of children and adolescents. Secondly, only studies from the United Kingdom are included. This is principally because it is difficult, and potentially misleading, to generalise from findings of research undertaken in other countries, where overall living conditions may differ, and where the composition and history of minority ethnic groups may be vastly different from those living in the UK. Thirdly, it only examines studies looking at the rates of mental health problems in those from minority ethnic groups. It does not include research on provision or use of services. Fourthly, the needs of refugee children are not specifically addressed in this chapter. They are dealt with elsewhere (Chapter 5). For the purpose of this chapter, the term 'ethnic minority group' is taken to mean the non-White minority groups, because most of the research available has focused on these groups, to the exclusion of others such as those of White European origin.

Epidemiological research – potential and pitfalls
General issues

Epidemiology has been described as the study of 'the pattern of diseases (and health, though usually indirectly) in populations to help understand both their causes and the burden they impose'. This information is applied to prevent, control or manage the problems under study (Bhopal 2002, p.xxii). In the specific context that we are discussing, this means the search for answers to the whether and the why. *Whether* children and adolescents from particular minority ethnic groups have higher or lower rates of mental health problems and, if they do, *why* this may be the case. Epidemiological research of this kind has been criticised on a number of grounds (Bhopal 1997; Chaturvedi 2001; Senior and Bhopal 1994), and some of these issues will be discussed later in this section. However, there are potential benefits in undertaking this kind of research. Three key potential benefits are listed below.

Knowledge of prevalence of mental health problems in different groups can allow for wiser provision of services to address those problems.

If specific differences in prevalence across ethnic groups exist, it can allow some understanding of the possible causes (aetiology) of specific mental health problems. If differences exist, it allows inequities to be addressed (Chaturvedi 2001; Senior and Bhopal 1994).

So, the potential benefits are clear. However, there are pitfalls in the conduct and interpretation of research in this area. These fall into two main groups – those problems particular to cross-cultural research (and particularly cross-cultural research of mental health problems), and those problems applicable to all epidemiological research.

Pitfalls in researching this particular area

Although much has been written about the problems of cross-cultural epidemiological research (Bhopal 1997; Chaturvedi 2001; Senior and Bhopal 1994), for the purposes of summarising, the pitfalls fall into two main groups – problems of definition and problems of meaning. (For those requiring further detail, references are provided in the resources section at the end.)

Problems of definition

Ethnicity is a complex categorisation, incorporating a mix of cultural heritage and practices, religious and other beliefs, language and race. The composition of the different ethnic groups in the UK and some of the difficulties of using ethnic categorisations in research have been described in Chapter 1. The problems inherent in classification by ethnic group will not be repeated here; however, it is worth briefly considering some of the implications of these difficulties. Although there are no perfect solutions, the way in which these issues are approached is important to consider when looking at research in this field. It presents a particular problem when considering the generalisability of a piece of research, both horizontal (across people) and vertical (across time). The way in which a piece of research may apply to a different group of individuals is important to consider with any piece of research (see 'Generalisability' below). However, even greater care should be taken in extrapolating from a study on one ethnic group across to another, though it may be very tempting to do so. For example, the study of children of Gujarati origin undertaken by Hackett and colleagues (Hackett, Hackett and Taylor 1991) gives information specifically about that community, and should not be taken as an example which can be extrapolated across other groups of Indian origin. Interpretation of research involving minority ethnic groups in the more distant past is also prone to difficulty. For example, Rutter and colleagues

(Rutter, Yule, Berger, Yule, Morton and Bagley 1974) studied children of West Indian origin in the early 1970s and drew conclusions about their behaviour at home and at school, relative to White children. These conclusions would be unlikely to be drawn if the same study were undertaken today, as not only has society in general changed, but the composition of minority ethnic groups has changed enormously in the 30 years since that particular piece of research was undertaken.

Problems of meaning

How applicable are diagnoses of mental illness across cultures? For the purposes of reviewing the epidemiological research, it is necessary to appreciate that there are large pitfalls in assuming that methods of describing mental health or ill health are applicable across ethnic groups. Words to describe symptoms may have very different meanings in different cultures, and may indicate a very different level of distress or disability from that seen in the 'White' UK population. The meaning in one ethnic group cannot necessarily be extrapolated to another, or even across all members of an ethnic group. Any extrapolations from symptoms to categories of mental illness or ill-health are vulnerable to distortions and should be interpreted with appropriate caution.

This leads to additional problems when measurement of symptoms is undertaken, particularly when symptoms are measured by brief questionnaires, as the meanings cannot be explored fully and so misunderstanding is more likely to occur. Many studies undertake translation and back translation of the questionnaires to try and ensure equivalence of their questionnaire in different languages (that is they translate the questionnaire into the second language and then translate it back into English to ensure that the correct words are used). While this does help to ensure grammatical accuracy, it does not ensure accuracy of meaning, as the words used and particularly the way in which they are used affects the meaning (Bird 1996). De Jong (2001) has outlined some of the issues requiring consideration for research tools to be useful in different ethnic or cultural groups — these include content validity, semantic validity, concept validity, technical validity and criterion validity (see also Kramer and Hodes 2003 for some discussion of these issues). These problems may lead to significant bias in the results, as particular symptoms may be over- or under-reported depending on the way in which they are asked about. The problem of different interpretations of questions has been demonstrated on internationally used questionnaires of physical symptoms, leading to wide differences in understanding (e.g. Fischbacher, Bhopal, Unwin, White, Alberti 2001). These differences may be more extreme when mental health issues are being inquired about. These difficulties have been demonstrated to have a significant effect on the outcome of results of research studies (Stone and Campbell 1984) – particularly when the area enquired about is a sensitive one, as mental health is for some people.

More general pitfalls for epidemiological studies

Studies of the mental health of children and adolescents from ethnic minorities are also vulnerable to the methodological pitfalls affecting all epidemiological research. These are summarised briefly below. Further details are available from any good epidemiology textbook (e.g. Hennekens and Buring 1987).

SELECTION BIAS

This occurs when the way in which the sample is selected leads to them not being representative of the population as a whole, or where the different groups being studied are not selected in the same way. For example, bias can occur when the two groups being studied are not recruited from the same place – for example, where one ethnic group is predominantly referred by parents and another ethnic group is predominantly referred by school. Differences found in a study doing this may be due to the different referral source rather than due to real differences between the ethnic groups.

OBSERVER BIAS

There are two types of observer bias. **Interviewer bias** could occur where the interviewer conducting the study responds in a different way to different groups within the study. It could occur, for example, if a teacher was rating children in their class for behavioural difficulties and the teacher had a pre-existing belief that children from one ethnic group were more likely to have behavioural problems than children from other ethnic groups. It can occur even where the interviewer makes a conscious effort to avoid it. It can be avoided by blinding the interviewer or rater to which group the subjects of the research are in. This is not possible in research of different ethnic groups. **Recall bias** can occur when the subject of the interview is more likely to recall something because of the nature of their condition. While a significant problem in many research projects, it is less likely to be a problem for research in this area.

VALIDITY OF THE MEASURES

This is probably one of the most important limitations of research examining differences in mental health problems in different ethnic groups. Most of the measures used are questionnaires, which have been developed or derived from White populations in the UK or the United States. Very few have been redeveloped involving other ethnic groups, and so the question of cross-cultural applicability applies, to a greater or lesser extent, to most of the measures used. This may have a significant impact on the validity of the research. It is difficult to accurately quantify the extent of this problem.

CONFOUNDING

This occurs where a third factor is related to both the outcome of the research and to the exposure being studied (in our case ethnicity). A common example of a confounder is social class, which in some studies is different in the different ethnic groups. Therefore, any differences found may be partly attributable to the confounding factor (e.g. social class) rather than due to differences in ethnicity.

GENERALISABILITY

When examining a piece of research, a judgement must be made as to how relevant it is to the population in which you are interested. There has already been reference made to the difficulties in extrapolating research from one ethnic group in one country, to another related but different ethnic group in another country. This is the generalisability or **external validity** of the research. Again there is not a ready way to quantify this, and it is a matter of fine judgement.

While the list of general and specific pitfalls above is not exhaustive, it covers the main points of concern when evaluating research. The judgements to be made are rarely clear cut. We have provided a suggested checklist below to assist the reader in assessing research in the field of ethnicity and mental health problems. It is adapted from the checklists developed by Sackett, Straus, Richardson, Rosenburg, Haynes (2000).

---

1.   Are subjects from different ethnic groups recruited in the same way?

2.   Are the groups similar in all respects apart from ethnicity (are there confounding factors)?

3.   Were all the subjects assessed in as consistent a way as possible?

4.   Have the measures used (e.g. questionnaires) been appropriately developed and validated in the different ethnic groups?

5.   Are any differences found by the research clinically significant and meaningful, rather than just statistically significant?

6.   Are the ethnic categorisations used relevant to the populations that I see in my area (are the results really generalisable)?

Box 3.1 Suggested questions to ask when examining cross-cultural epidemiological research

What research is there?

The available research on ethnicity and mental health has focused predominantly on the adult population, and also on conditions that seem to have presented more frequently in minority ethnic populations (notably schizophrenia in African-Caribbean men), rather than those that are less common in the minority ethnic populations, and so commoner in the 'White' population. This is not unique to mental health research, as it occurs across the range of health problems encompassing conditions such as diabetes and coronary heart disease (Hopkins and Bahl 1993; Smaje 1995). The accuracy of the picture generated by this research has been questioned (Nazroo 1997), and it has served to increase the focus on differences in health needs, rather than the greater similarities that exist. It has resulted in an evidence base regarding the mental health needs of children and adolescents from minority ethnic groups that is far from clear and even further from being comprehensive.

There has been very little epidemiological research conducted examining ethnicity and mental health in children and adolescents in the UK. Many of the books addressing the health care and/or mental health care of minority ethnic groups make small reference to the needs of children and adolescents (Bhugra and Bahl 1999; Bhugra and Cochrane 2001; BMA 1995). The aim of the following section is to summarise and discuss the most significant pieces of research that have been conducted. This includes the larger epidemiological studies conducted.

The first interest in differences between the mental health of the indigenous White population and those from ethnic minorities in the UK surfaced in the 1960s, with more research being published later. Michael Rutter and colleagues (Rutter *et al.* 1974) studied 116 ten-year-old children of West Indian origin in Inner London in 1970. Their mothers were interviewed at home by either a Black (34 families) or a White (66 families) interviewer, using a standardised interview. Their school teachers were also interviewed.

The study describes comparisons between the West Indian origin children and a control group (referred to as the 'non-immigrant group') of similar age. The West Indian children were found to have higher rates of 'behavioural deviance' (including restlessness, poor concentration and socially disapproved conduct) on a questionnaire completed by their teachers, but no difference with regard to emotional difficulties. The 'non-immigrant' children had higher rates of truancy and school absence. When the teacher interview data was used, the West Indian children had higher rates of conduct problems but there were no statistically significant differences between the groups for overall levels of disorder.

The higher rates of 'behavioural deviance' reported by the teachers in West Indian children were not confirmed by parent report. While it is inevitable that the age of this research limits its applicability to the UK now, there are several other questions that arise when considering this research. It is puzzling that the higher rates of conduct problems reported in school are not reported by parents, suggesting either different behaviour at school or some systematic bias in the way that children were assessed by their teacher. The possibility that teachers had an inherent bias in the way they were viewing children from different backgrounds was considered by the authors. There was little discussion of the finding that non-immigrant children had higher rates of truancy and school absence than West Indian origin children – it is commonly found in cross-cultural research that higher rates of disorder in the non-White group are highlighted whereas lower rates, which may signify some improved health or functioning, are not discussed.

Goodman and Richards (1995) conducted a study designed to compare the mental health of children from different ethnic backgrounds. They examined the case notes from the Maudsley Hospital (a psychiatric hospital) in South London from the years 1973–1989. This is the same institution as that where the previously described research (Rutter *et al.* 1974) was conducted. Goodman and Richards compared the notes of 292 second generation immigrant children (mostly but not exclusively African-Caribbean in origin), with 1311 White children. The White children were predominantly referred by their parent or GP (47 per cent versus 23 per cent from education), whereas the second generation immigrant children were more commonly referred by the education services (31 per cent from parents or GP versus 36 per cent from education). Goodman and Richards found similar differences between the second generation immigrants and the non-immigrant children as had been found by Rutter and colleagues' earlier study. The second generation immigrant children (predominantly African-Caribbean) had higher rates of conduct problems, and the much rarer psychotic and autistic conditions, but lower rates of emotional problems. While this can be viewed as some confirmation of the earlier 1974 study, there are some important possibilities of bias to consider. The issue of referral bias is considered by the authors, as is the problem of only researching children referred to a specialist institution, so limiting the generalisability of the findings to the wider population. As well as these potential biases, the possibility of bias in the diagnoses made by the psychiatrists at the Maudsley hospital over the time of the study (1973–1989) must be considered. It is possible that they had pre-existing beliefs about the rates of disorders occurring in different ethnic groups, partly because they were working at the institution where the original 1974 research was conducted. No information is given as to the ethnicity of the psychiatrists working there.

Cochrane (1979) sent Rutter Children's Behaviour Questionnaires to the teachers of nine-year-old children in five schools in Birmingham, which had been selected for their ethnic diversity. Three hundred and nineteen questionnaires were completed, and children were analysed according to the place of birth of their parents (India, Pakistan, the West Indies or Britain). The average scores on the questionnaires showed slightly lower scores for the 'Pakistani' children than for the other groups, with the 'British' group scoring the highest. However, when the standard cut-off score was used to identify behavioural deviance, no significant differences were found between the groups. As with the previous studies, there are concerns about the validity of some of the findings, given that a screening questionnaire was used, definitive rates of mental health problems cannot be identified. It is interesting that contrasting results were found compared to the study by Rutter and colleagues (1974). Whether this is due to a difference in time, the place in which the study was conducted or random variation, we do not know.

There has been less published research focusing on ethnic groups of Asian origin in the UK. Hackett et al. (1991) recruited 200 mothers of children aged between four and seven years from schools and community contacts in Oldham and Ashton-under-Lyme. Half the sample were from the East Manchester Gujarati community and half from what they describe as an 'English' sample from the same area. All mothers were interviewed using a standard questionnaire (Rutter A2 questionnaire) in either English, Hindi or Gujarati, depending on parental preference. Using this questionnaire, they found that 21 per cent of the 'English' children were rated as disturbed (6 per cent emotional disorder, 13 per cent conduct disorder, 2 per cent mixed disorder), and 5 per cent of the 'Gujarati' children were disturbed (3 per cent emotional disorder, 2 per cent conduct disorder). The authors speculate that these differences in rates of disturbance may be to do with a more intact family structure and different cultural practices (including child rearing practices) in the Gujarati group. However, no details are given of the method of translation of the questionnaire, and it is acknowledged that it has not been validated in the Gujarati community. Care should be taken in considering these results – particularly if trying to extrapolate them to apply beyond the original Manchester Gujarati community.

In 1999 the Office of National Statistics carried out a national survey of the mental health of children and adolescents (aged 5 to 15 years) across Great Britain (Melzer, Gatward, Goodman, Ford 2000). Although it was not specifically designed with the aim of investigating mental health problems in minority ethnic groups, because of the scale and scope of the undertaking, it represented an opportunity to examine some of these issues. It was a survey of over 10,000 children and adolescents. The majority of children and their parent(s) were interviewed and their teacher also contacted to complete a postal questionnaire. In most cases, parents were interviewed face to face. The measures used included the Strengths and Difficulties questionnaire (SDQ), and a newly designed interview measure. Where parents did not have a sufficient grasp of English, a self-completion version of the SDQ was given to them.

The study reported that 10 per cent of White, 12 per cent of Black, 8 per cent of Pakistani and Bangladeshi and 4 per cent of Indian children were assessed as having a mental health problem. However, because of the relatively small numbers of children involved from minority ethnic groups, the authors caution against interpreting these as statistically meaningful differences between the ethnic groups. They do suggest that Indian children had lower rates of mental disorder than White or Black children.

However, a number of issues require consideration before the results can be accepted at face value. The principal concerns relate to the possibility of bias within the study – particularly related to the minority ethnic groups. There is a possibility of selection bias if a disproportionate number of those opting out of the study were from non-White groups. Unfortunately, there is no way of accurately assessing this. The questionnaires used, including the SDQ, have not been validated in many of the ethnic groups interviewed, and so the comparability of the answers given is called into question. In addition, those who could not speak sufficient English (numbers not specified) were given a self-completion questionnaire rather than being interviewed, as all the other subjects were. This may have affected the responses given and is likely to have happened more to those from non-White ethnic groups. Finally the ethnic categorisations used are of concern. While some shorthand categorisation is inevitable in a large survey, different ethnic groups (e.g. Black, or Pakistani and Bangladeshi) were grouped together in order to allow sufficient numbers in these subgroups. These caveats should be borne in mind when considering the results of this study.

Conclusions

Conducting research in this field is extremely difficult, and the studies outlined above, despite their limitations, represent the most significant attempts to do this in the UK. The most noticeable thing about the state of research in this field is the paucity of it. Important questions, which epidemiology could make a contribution to answering, are being left unanswered because of a lack of research impetus.

Summarising the available research presents a difficulty. This is partly because there have been but a handful of studies over 30 years, during which time ethnic groups and the concept and understanding of ethnicity has evolved enormously in this country. It is also because the potential biases and problems with the research limit the extent to which conclusions can confidently be drawn. It may be that there are differential rates of mental health problems in different ethnic groups in this country. If there are, then the most likely differences demonstrated by the research (because of the relative consistency with which they are found) are that children whose ethnic identity is linked with the Indian subcontinent have lower overall rates of mental health problems as a group. The findings of higher rates of behavioural problems in children categorised as having Black West Indian ethnicity have not been confirmed in the studies in Birmingham, nor by the nationwide survey, and so the research supporting this in the UK comes from one institution in South London. However, I would suggest, and it is a personal interpretation, that the research base to date does not sufficiently support these conclusions for them to be definite, without replication of these findings in other parts of the UK and in other ethnic groups. It is important to remember that even if differences of rates of problems exist between groups, they are likely to be small differences, and at a local level the similarities in presentation between individuals are going to be greater than the differences.

It seems likely that a more fruitful way ahead lies in working with specific groups in local areas to determine, with them, their mental health needs. This will benefit from the use of a variety of research methods, including insights from epidemiology, but also using more detailed individual information derived from qualitative research methods. The adaptation of epidemiological methods to do this is undoubtedly more difficult and resource-consuming, but without such efforts, valid and useful answers from research are less likely to be forthcoming. Until such research is undertaken, serious questions will remain as to whether the mental health needs of minority ethnic children and adolescents are being met.

References

Bhopal, R. (1997) 'Is research into ethnicity and health racist, unsound, or important science?' *British Medical Journal 314*, 1751.

Bhopal, R.S. (2002) *Concepts of Epidemiology: An integrated introduction to the ideas, theories, principles, and methods of epidemiology.* Oxford: Oxford University Press.

Bhugra, D. and Bahl, V. (1999) *Ethnicity: An Agenda for Mental Health.* London: Gaskell.

Bhugra, D. and Cochrane, R. (2001) *Psychiatry in Multi-Cultural Britain.* London: Gaskell.

Bird, H.R. (1996) 'Epidemiology of childhood disorders in a cross-cultural context.' *Journal of Child Psychology and Psychiatry 37*, 35–39.

British Medical Association (1995) *Multicultural Health Care.* London: British Medical Association.

Chaturvedi, N. (2001) 'Ethnicity as an epidemiological determinant – crudely racist or crucially important?' *International Journal of Epidemiology 30*, 925–927.

Cochrane, R. (1979) 'Psychological and behavioural disturbance in West Indians, Indians and Pakistanis in Britain: A comparison of rates among children and adults.' *British Journal of Psychiatry 134*, 201–210.

De Jong, J. (2001) Annual meeting of the Royal College of Psychiatrists, London.

Fischbacher, C.M., Bhopal, R., Unwin, N., White, M. and Alberti, K.G. (2001) 'The performance of the Rose angina questionnaire in South Asian and European origin populations: a comparative study in Newcastle, UK.' *International Journal of Epidemiology 30*, 1009–1016.

Goodman, R. and Richards, H. (1995) 'Child and Adolescent Psychiatric Presentations of Second-Generation Afro-Caribbeans in Britain.' *British Journal of Psychiatry 167*, 362–369.

Hackett, R., Hackett, L. and Taylor, D.C. (1991) 'Psychological disturbance and its associations in the children of the Gujarati community.' *Journal of Child Psychology and Psychiatry 32*, 851–856.

Hennekens, C.H. and Buring, J.E. (1987) *Epidemiology in Medicine.* Philadelphia, PA: Lippincott Williams and Wilkins.

Hopkins, A. and Bahl, V. (1993) *Access to health care for people from black and ethnic minorities.* London: Royal College of Physicians of London.

Kramer, T. and Hodes, M. (2003) 'The Mental Health of British Afro-Caribbean children and adolescents.' In D. Ndegwa and D. Olajide (eds) *Main Issues in Mental Health and Race.* Aldershot: Ashgate Press.

Meltzer, H., Gatward, R., Goodman, R. and Ford, T. (2000) *Mental Health of Children and Adolescents in Great Britain.* London: The Stationary Office.

Nazroo, J. (1997) *Ethnicity and Mental Health: Findings from a National Community Survey.* London: Policy Studies Institute.

Rutter, M., Yule, W., Berger, M., Yule, B., Morton, J. and Bagley, C. (1974) 'Children of West Indian immigrants – I. Rates of behavioural deviance and of psychiatric disorder.' *Journal of Child Psychology and Psychiatry 15*, 241–262.

Sackett, D., Straus, S., Richardson, W.S., Rosenberg, W. and Haynes, R.B. (2000) *Evidence-Base Medicine – How to practice and teach EBM.* London: Churchill Livingstone.

Senior, P. and Bhopal, R.S. (1994) 'Ethnicity as a variable in epidemiological research.' *British Medical Journal 309*, 327–329.

Smaje, C. (1995) *Health, 'Race' and Ethnicity: Making Sense of the Evidence.* London: Kings Fund Institute.

Stone, L. and Campbell, J.G. (1984) 'The use and misuse of surveys in international development: an experiment from Nepal.' *Human Organisations 43*, 27–37.

Further reading

Balajaran, R. and Soni Raleigh, V. (1995) *Ethnicity and Health in England.* London: HMSO.

Brewin, C. (1980) 'Explaining the lower rates of psychiatric treatment among Asian immigrants to the United Kingdom: a preliminary study.' *Social Psychiatry 15*, 17–19.

Bui, K.V-T. and Takeuchi, D.T. (1992) 'Ethnic minority adolescents and the use of community mental health care services.' *American Journal of Community Psychology 20*, 403–417.

Cooper, H., Smaje, C. and Arber, S. (1998) 'Use of health services by children and young people according to ethnicity and social class: secondary analysis of a national survey.' *British Medical Journal 317*, 1047–1051.

Jawed, S. (1991) 'A survey of psychiatrically ill Asian children.' *Psychiatric Bulletin 158*, 268–270.

Lipsedge, M. (1993) Mental Health: access to care for black and ethnic minority people. In A. Hopkins and V. Bahl (eds) *Access to health care for people from black and ethnic minorities*, 169–186 London: Royal College of Physicians of London.

Nikapota, A.D. (2001) 'Child Psychiatry.' In D. Bhugra and R. Cochrane (eds) *Psychiatry in Multicultural Britain*, 191–210. London: Gaskell.

OPCS (1994) *1991 census: children and young adults. Vol. 1.* London: HMSO.

Pumariega, A.J., Glover, S., Holzer, C.E. 3rd and Nguyen, H. (1998) 'II. Utilization of mental health services in a tri-ethnic sample of adolescents.' *Community Mental Health Journal 34*, 145–156.

Stern, G., Cottrell, D. and Holmes, J. (1990) 'Patterns of attendance of child psychiatry outpatients with special reference to Asian families.' *British Journal of Psychiatry 156*, 384–387.

4 Meeting the Needs of Minority Ethnic Groups in the UK

Mhemooda Malek

As stated in the introduction to this report, one of the principles high-lighted in recent NHS reforms is to ensure equal access to health services for all people. A number of other legislative, policy and practice guide-lines promote the need for greater equality, some of these having implica-tions for health provision either directly or indirectly. People from minority ethnic groups are specifically highlighted in, or are the main focus of, a number of such documents (see Box 4.1).

The introduction of legislation and reforms is a step in the right direc-tion if their intentions can be translated into action. Though there is a greater focus on addressing needs of minority ethnic groups than has pre-viously been the case, it is suggested that some issues, such as those relating to access, have received insufficient attention in the restructuring of the NHS (Bhui, Christie and Bhugra 1995). Inability to access services can be a significant factor contributing to the presentation of difficulties at the point of crisis.

Bhui *et al.* (1995) highlight that cultural issues can pose insurmount-able barriers to the provision of an appropriate mental health service. Overcoming them requires not only that issues are better understood but also that substantial alterations to the service are made. Measures taken to address the needs of minority ethnic groups are unlikely to succeed if the structural components of a comprehensive mental health service are

- **The Patients Charter** highlights a commitment to providing mental health services for minority groups and these should respect privacy, dignity, religious and cultural beliefs.

- **The Health of the Nation** indicates that in considering action to achieve targets, the particular needs of people from minority ethnic groups should be taken into account.

- **The Race Relations Act 1976** states that services have a duty not to discriminate on the grounds of race and should be provided in a manner that is appropriate and acceptable to all ethnic groups.

- **The Race Relations Amendment Act 2000** extends the scope of the 1976 Act by making this duty enforceable. Under this Act, Public Bodies can be held accountable in a court of law for not enforcing the duty. In the NHS, Public Bodies are defined as Health Authorities, Health Boards, NHS Trusts and Primary Care Trusts.

Box 4.1: Key documents relating to minority ethnic groups

absent. Services should be local, accessible, comprehensive, flexible, consumer-oriented, empowering clients, focusing on strengths, normalised and incorporate natural supports, able to meet special needs, accountable and culturally appropriate.

Figure 4.1 summarises some of the key issues acting as barriers to care which children from minority ethnic groups may experience.

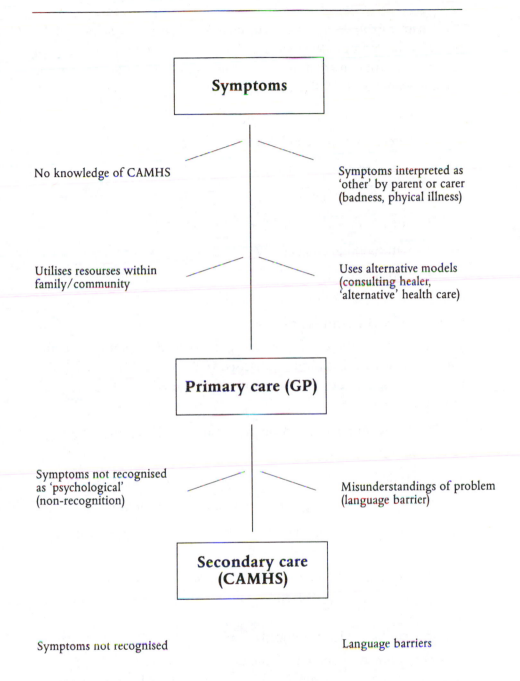

Figure 4.1 *Potential barriers to care (adapted from Goldberg and Huxley (1980) pathways to care model)*

This chapter explores in more detail some key factors that impact on the provision of appropriate services and act as barriers to accessing such services for children from minority ethnic groups. The factors will be considered under the following headings:

- Planning and commissioning.

- Perceptions of mental illness.

- Client perceptions of services.

- Access to services.

- The delivery of culturally sensitive services.

- Staff training/competency.

- Evaluation.

Planning and commissioning

The relevance of the commissioning process to developing culturally competent services has been emphasised (Bahl 1998; Bhui *et al.* 1995; Rawaf 1998). The broad components highlighted as relevant to this process include:

- the use of relevant information about local minority ethnic groups

- taking account of minority ethnic groups in needs assessments

- regular monitoring and review of quality standards

- specifying to providers the delivery of culturally competent services

- developing the involvement of the voluntary sector in planning and provision.

Information about local minority ethnic groups

A lack of information about local minority ethnic groups has been previously cited by some commissioners as a major obstacle to the development of policy and provision to address needs (Office for Public Management 1996). Others were of the opinion that national sources could rea-

FOCUS Survey (Part 2)

Few commissioners had up-to-date information about the minority ethnic groups in their area in relation to:

- minority ethnic groups' awareness of mental health issues
- minority ethnic groups' awareness of mental health services
- minority ethnic groups' access to services
- the types of services used
- discrepencies in the types of services used.

sonably indicate local needs. The nature of information referred to included a range of areas including profiles of minority ethnic mortality and morbidity.

The Office for Public Management (1996) study noted that organisational changes preoccupying commissioners were cited as a major reason for the limited attention given to addressing health needs of minority ethnic groups. It is suggested that consideration about meeting the needs of minority ethnic groups should be part of mainstream organisational processes and not seen as an 'add on' (Bahl 1998; Bhui *et al.* 1995).

It is important to review the data collection systems in place to record information relating to minority ethnic groups. If adequate systems are not in place it will not be possible to review progress made in meeting the needs of this population. The data needs to be sufficiently detailed to allow services to identify different minority ethnic groups as some service changes may have differing effects on local populations.

Needs assessments

Significant emphasis is given to the importance of undertaking needs assessments in relation to both child and adolescent mental health (Health Advisory Service 1995) and health needs of the general population (Secretary of State for Health 1997). Needs assessments are described as a vital aspect of the commissioning process to address the needs of local populations. Considering particular needs such as those of minority ethnic groups is an important aspect of this process (Rawaf 1998). It is also suggested that to be useful, needs assessments should be updated regularly to take account of changes in the structure of the local populations and their needs (Bahl 1998). Securing services that meet the needs of minority ethnic groups should be a core aspect of the commissioning process (Chandra 1996).

Factors that should be considered as part of the process of assessing population needs include:

- Within the overall estimation of population needs there should be some identification of minority ethnic groups to be targeted.

- Such an exercise should be incorporated into the planning process and repeated at regular intervals.

- Information systems should be developed to address issues such as the size of the local population, local vulnerabilities and indices of local deprivation as an essential component of the service.

FOCUS Survey (Part 2)

Of the 11 commissioners who cited sources they used to obtain profiles of local minority ethnic groups, 7 out of 11 said that they did not use this information systematically to plan service provision.

It is clear from the feedback of all participating commissioners that ethnicity as a component of CAMHS needs assessments requires significant development. Otherwise the capacity of services to develop provision that addresses the needs of minority ethnic groups is likely to be limited.

Clients from minority ethnic groups did not contribute to any of the planning and provision in 12 of 14 services.

Minority ethnic communities are often under-represented in decision-making positions and their involvement in needs assessments as well as policy and planning decisions is important (Bhui *et al.* 1995; Hardman and Harris 1998; Rawaf 1998). Services need to adopt a client-led approach and not be based on professional assumptions about what clients need.

Monitoring and review of quality standards

Setting quality standards for the health of minority ethnic groups, monitoring progress and taking forward findings highlighted by regular reviews are an essential component of ensuring high quality services, including the commissioning process (Rawaf 1998; Bahl 1998). Potential areas for standard setting and review may include mental health promotion, identification of mental health problems, assessment of mental health problems, the appropriateness of services to meet current needs and the effectiveness of interventions provided.

It is suggested that commissioners can support providers to understand and address the needs of local communities (Bahl 1998). One of the ways in which this can be achieved is by way of commissioners communicating the needs of local communities to providers in order to facilitate them in developing appropriate services.

FOCUS Survey (Part 2)

No regular reviews of service provision for minority ethnic groups were conducted by commissioners. There was an indication from some commissioners that general reviews *may* take into account service provision for minority ethnic groups.

Ten of the 11 commissioners who responded did not provide any guidelines to service providers about addressing the mental health needs of clients from minority ethnic groups.

Seven of the 11 commissioners who responded did not specify requirements in service specifications or contracts, about the provision of services to address the mental health needs of local minority ethnic groups.

Involvement of the voluntary sector

In addition to individual and community feedback, a multi-agency consultation forum is suggested as a useful approach to involving a range of clients, professionals and organisations (Bhui *et al.* 1995). Involvement of voluntary sector services is particularly highlighted. Such meetings should be held on a regular basis and especially at times of restructuring. The involvement of key players from the initial stages of planning is vital and should not be undertaken as an add-on or token gesture. A top down approach is described as being doomed to failure and will not address any mistrust and suspicion about mental health services (Bhugra 1993).

Services in the voluntary sector are increasingly acknowledged as key contributors in the provision of services to address mental health and well-being. Their important role is recognised in relation to CAMHS provision and in addressing the needs of minority ethnic groups. In their review of CAMHS, Kurtz, Thornes and Wolkind (1994) conclude that they found an impressive range of services being provided by the voluntary sector, across primary and specialist levels. The House of Commons Health Committee Report (1997) on CAMHS recommends that the Department of Health should encourage expansion of relevant voluntary sector initiatives and look at how their funding might be made more secure (para. 54). Bhui *et al.* (1995) highlight that one of the essential elements of psychiatric services for minority ethnic groups is to specify a local role for voluntary sector organisations.

There is no single or straightforward set of criteria that can be applied to defining the voluntary sector. Furthermore, boundaries between the public, private and voluntary sectors have become increasingly blurred with the introduction of a market economy and contract culture in the provision of welfare services. Voluntary sector agencies can now bid for contracts alongside public and private sector organisations, indeed sometimes in competition with them. Knight (1993) refers to this as the 'blurred sector hypothesis'.

Another term that lacks clarity is 'voluntary and community sector' and the terms 'voluntary' and 'community' are sometimes used interchangeably. In the context of provision that addresses health and welfare needs of clients, these terms appear to generally refer to non-statutory organisations, many of which are based in, and work with, local communities. In the absence of definitive criteria, a number of features that are usually associated with this sector are highlighted (Knight 1993):

- independent beginnings
- self-governing structures
- independence from other agencies
- independent financing
- use of volunteers
- distribution of surpluses not for profit
- worthwhile purpose.

These criteria are said to apply to voluntary sector organisations to varying degrees. The increasing dependence on statutory funding has, however, raised the question about the extent to which voluntary organisations are truly voluntary.

Innovative approaches to addressing needs have often been associated with the voluntary sector (Health Advisory Service 1995). With particular reference to CAMHS, Kurtz *et al.* (1994) have noted that in addition to undertaking significant work at the primary care level, voluntary organisations also act as a filter to specialist mental health and social services. It is also suggested that the potential contribution from this sector remains untapped and commissioning mechanisms should see its involvement as integral to planning and provision of services (Bahl 1998; Bhui *et al.* 1995) as well as being well placed to provide training for mental health professionals. It has been suggested that one of the essential elements of health provision, including psychiatric services, for minority ethnic groups is to specify a role for voluntary sector organisations (Bahl 1998; Bhui *et al.* 1995; Hardman and Harris 1998; Nadirshaw 1992).

In a report commissioned by the Kings Fund, Chandra (1996) highlights some features of voluntary organisations that contribute to relative success in working with minority ethnic groups:

- They are culturally competent, often providing services that are language and culture specific.

- They are knowledgeable about local communities and the factors impinging on individuals from those communities.

- They appear to be user-friendly and accessible.

- They can provide a vital link between clients and other services, including those in the statutory sector.

It has been suggested that mental health teams should be developed in each locality to:

- raise the profile of the needs of local minority ethnic groups

- act as a resource for other agencies

- contribute to the training of health care workers.

Singh (1998), in a Department of Health-funded study, highlights the need to see voluntary sector contributions as an integral part of provision. Health agencies should facilitate voluntary sector contribution to commissioning strategies that enable effective health service delivery to minority ethnic groups. Facilitating a more active role for the voluntary sector also requires recognising and addressing the constraints that agencies in this sector often work under (Bahl 1998; Webb-Johnson and Nadirshaw 1993). Factors such as lack of relevant information about NHS structures, insecure and inadequate funding, insufficient other

Recommendations

Regular needs assessments are conducted as part of the commissioning process and representatives from minority ethnic groups are involved in this process.

Voluntary sector organisations are actively involved in the commissioning process.

Quality standards are defined and evaluated.

Each CAMHS develops and implements a service delivery strategy for children and adolescents from minority ethnic groups.

resources such as staffing and equipment and the absence of relevant training and support are said to limit this sector from achieving its full potential.

Perceptions of mental illness

Individual perceptions and understanding about mental health and ill-health have a significant role in the identification of factors that impact on mental health and well-being. Both the client and the professional are significant players in this respect. A failure to recognise and understand factors that impact on mental health on either part is likely to minimise the effectiveness of assessment, diagnosis and subsequent access to relevant treatment and support (Bahl 1998; Bhui *et al.* 1995; Rawaf 1998). A number of studies highlight issues that impact on the effective recognition of mental health difficulties and relate to both professionals and clients.

Conceptualisation and expression of mental distress can vary across cultures (Bhugra and Cochrane 1997; Goldberg and Hodes 1992; Littlewood and Lipsedge 1997). A number of explanations have been proposed in relation to how minority ethnic groups in Britain might express, or otherwise deal with, mental distress and some of these have been subsequently challenged. Stereotypical approaches and a tendency to generalise without taking into account the hetrogeneity of minority ethnic people are at the heart of many criticisms. Studies in this country have largely tended to focus on 'South Asians' perceptions of mental health; they may nevertheless have relevance for other groups.

A frequent explanation given in relation to South Asians is that they are more prone to 'somaticising' mental states (Leff 1981). Other research highlights that expressions of mental distress are in fact vivid and include both somatic and psychological concepts, some of which have similarities to Western constructs of mental states, such as depression (Fenton and Sadig-Sangster 1996). Clients may have difficulty in expressing certain concepts to professionals who speak a different language to themselves; professionals on the other hand may not recognise the expression of distress if they are unfamiliar with the client's cultural context. In the absence of information on which a psychiatric diagnosis is usually made, doctors may be inclined to treat presenting symptoms as a primarily physical and not a psychological condition. Clients wishing to avoid the stigma of being treated for mental health concerns may be willing to readily accept such a diagnosis (Brewin 1980; Green *et al.* 2002). Furthermore there is no evidence to suggest that South Asians are more likely to somaticise than other minority or majority groups (Patel 2000).

It has also been suggested that 'Asian' parents are likely to tolerate a greater range of behaviours, contributing to the low numbers of referrals of this group to CAMHS (Stern, Cottrell and Holmes 1990). Hackett and Hackett (1993) raise the important question of whether the parents' standards, or Western standards of what is acceptable, should be used as a yardstick.

Another explanation offered in relation to fewer South Asian families being represented in CAMHS is that the young people of these families have more secure foundations than others (Bourne 1990). However, this is challenged by the larger numbers that attend when services are made accessible and appropriate (Hardman and Harris 1998; Jayarajan 2001).

Another frequently cited barrier in relation to minority ethnic groups recognising or seeking treatment for mental health difficulties is stigma. However, there is no conclusive evidence to support the view that minority ethnic groups perceive mental health difficulties to be more stigmatising than other groups (Patel 2000).

These examples illustrate that while some factors may have relevance for individuals, there is a need to guard against assuming that they are more applicable to some groups than others. Understanding individuals and their cultural context is likely to be a more productive approach than generalising on the basis of stereotypical approaches and in the absence of conclusive evidence.

Knowledge about the social and cultural context of individuals and their communities is relevant to understanding how they might perceive and express mental distress. It is also relevant to health promotion where consideration should be given to how communications are likely to be understood by those at whom they are targeted (Webb 1996).

> ## Recommendations
>
> Initiatives are developed to communicate with local minority ethnic communities to encourage them to access services.

Client perceptions of services

The suggestion that people from minority ethnic groups do not wish or need to use mental health services is not supported by either the increased attendance in provision that is seen to be appropriate or in parental feedback concerning use of services (Fatemilehin and Coleman 1999; Hardman and Harris 1998; Messent and Murrell 2003).

A range of factors are highlighted as barriers that might prevent people from minority ethnic groups using primary care and mental health provision. Some of the available literature focuses on particular minority ethnic groups and messages are highlighted from studies looking at a wide range of age groups as well as those focused particularly on young people (Beliappa 1991; Fatemilehin and Coleman 1999; Hardman and Harris 1998; Messent and Murrell 2003; Webb-Johnson and Nadirshaw 1993).

Fear of racism

The experience of racism may influence client perception of mental health services and the professionals within it as being part of a wider racist society. The stage of the migratory process and degree of acculturation may also have some influence on the uptake of services, as could clients' own contexts and beliefs about dealing with mental health problems. Social, economic and political experience may also be relevant to client perceptions about mental health provision (Boyd-Franklin 1989; O'Brian 1990; Messent 1992).

Lack of awareness of service provision

A study commissioned by the Department of Health (Arber 2000) concluded that a lack of information about the NHS, its organisational structure and mode of operation were cited by general practitioners and parents as a barrier to receiving appropriate health care for young people. It is suggested that this contributes to a lower uptake of other primary and preventive services.

Studies looking at Bangladeshi and African Caribbean parent views, with particular reference to statutory mental health provision, highlight that this lack of awareness can relate to a number of factors. Messent and Murrell (2003) obtained feedback from Bangladeshi parents attending a CAMHS service in East London about why they thought Bangladeshi clients on the whole were under-represented in the service. The authors acknowledge the potential bias in relation to the involvement of clients already attending the service and highlight the need for this approach as a useful starting point in trying to understand significant under use of the service by this group. Bangladeshi parents participating in the study gave the following views:

- The lack of self-referrals was not seen as an indication that Bangladeshi families had fewer problems, rather that this was due to a lack of knowledge and information about the service. This view was also reflected in feedback obtained from other helping professionals working with Bangladeshi clients.

- Signposting to the service was seen as poor, making the service 'invisible'.

- Bangladeshi families were unlikely to be familiar with this kind of specialist support. Stern et al. (1990) have also suggested that there are virtually no psychiatric services in the area of Bangladesh from where most of the Bangladeshi community of East London have migrated. As a result Bangladeshi parents may not perceive psychiatric services to be of use.

A number of suggestions were made by parents in this study as to how the lack of awareness could be addressed:

- Awareness of the service could be raised through displaying information in community settings such as health centres and mosques.

- CAMHS staff could attend open days at venues frequented by the Bangladeshi community such as schools and mosques.

- The CAMHS service could be advertised via the local media such as newspapers and radio stations.

Fatemilehin and Coleman (1999) obtained the views of African Caribbean parents in relation to clinical psychology services for young people. Their responses highlight that there was little awareness about:

- clinical psychology services

- how they were provided

- how to gain access

- the difference between psychology and psychiatry – for some any difference was not relevant.

Lack of confidence in the services' ability to help

A lack of confidence in the ability of services to address the needs of minority groups is highlighted as a significant barrier in the pathway to accessing support. Anane-Agyei, Lobatto and Messent (2002) highlight the perception held by some African parents that many agencies represent White culture and lack understanding about values and ways of raising children in other cultures. The authors comment that, in turn, this wariness is interpreted by professionals as an unwillingness on the part of families to co-operate. A negative cycle is established with both sides feeling their negative beliefs about each other are borne out.

The parents in Fatemilehin and Coleman's (1999) study also indicated that use of mental health provision would be impeded by clients feeling disempowered. In order to make use of provision, parents would need some assurance that services would offer:

- confidentiality

- self-referral – some parents did not see referral via the GP as appropriate

- a non-stigmatising environment

- access to Black psychologists who were able to practise from a non-Eurocentric knowledge base. Some participants were willing to see a White psychiatrist who had a clear understanding of issues affecting Black people, highlighting the importance of choice.

Problems with language

Language has been highlighted as a factor that may affect clients' ability to access services. Cohen (2000) found that for families where migration was recent and English was not fluent, there could be increased difficulties in accessing primary care services. This has implications for subsequent referral to specialist services such as CAMHS because primary care can be the gateway to other support. Parents whose first language was not English reported that they dreaded using child health services due to the frustration of communication. Language and communication issues are considered in more detail on (p.132).

Recommendations

Services should devise relevant strategies for communicating with local minority ethnic groups to inform them of the nature and range of services available.

Access to services

Referral pathways for particular minority ethnic groups

Differences in referral pathways to CAMHS for particular ethnic groups are also apparent; however, the studies are not consistent in their findings for particular groups. The variations in studies may be due to heterogeneity of client groups and in the culture of particular services with regard to how they address cultural diversity of their client groups. Demographic and social factors impinging on individuals and communities may also be significant contributors to variations.

Daryanani, Hindley, Evans, Fahy, Turk (2001) found a statistically significant bias in relation to the referral route to CAMHS and ethnicity of children; the referral process varied by profession. The authors define subcategories included in broad ethnic categories, such as 'Black', and acknowledge the limitations of collapsing subcategories for the purpose of statistical analysis. Their approach nevertheless identified an over-referral of:

- White children by GPs
- Black children by specialist doctors and education services ('Black' includes African, Black Caribbean, Black British and Black Other)
- South Asian children by specialist doctors ('South Asian' includes Indian, Pakistani and Bangladeshi)
- dual heritage children by social services.

The authors suggest that differences in referral routes may be appropriate or inappropriate. If appropriate then one explanation could be that there are genuine differences in morbidity leading to presentation to different referrers. If inappropriate then the reasons might be client-related or service-related factors that influence referral practices. For example, parents' perception of problem and personal preference are likely to influence choice of referrer. Referrers (other professionals) may have biases in relation to definition of problems, their experience of CAMHS, and their own ethnic and cultural location. It is also suggested that the issue of racism on the educational opportunities of pupils from minority ethnic groups has not been addressed. The emotional and behavioural problems highlighted in children from minority ethnic groups in school may be a consequence of racism and result in their being excluded or referred to a CAMHS. In relation to children of dual heritage, the authors highlight the disproportionate number of these children being referred by social services, as a reflection of their over-representation in the social services looked-after system.

Kramer, Evans and Garralda (2000), in their study of referrals to a CAMHS, found that modification of Census categories revealed important patterns in relation to service use. They compared all minority ethnic groups with White counterparts as well as particular minority ethnic groups with White counterparts and found significant differences in referral agent and referral problems.

COMPARISON WITH WHITE UK AND ALL MINORITY ETHNIC GROUPS

- Young people from minority ethnic groups were more likely to be referred by primary care health services and to self-refer than their White counterparts. This contradicts other findings that minority ethnic groups are less likely to be referred by primary care (Commander, Sashidharan, Odell, Surtees 1997; Minnis, Kelly, Bradby submitted). Anane-Agyei *et al.* (2002) found that African children were less likely to self-refer to CAMHS.

- Young people from minority ethnic groups were less likely to be referred by secondary services and the most common reason for referral in this group was poor parenting.

- Fewer young people from minority ethnic groups were referred for developmental problems but more were diagnosed with a developmental disorder following assessment.

- There was a trend for non-White children to have more functional somatic symptoms (such as headaches, abdominal pain).

COMPARISON OF WHITE UK WITH INDIVIDUAL MINORITY ETHNIC GROUPS

- **Dual heritage** young people **with one UK parent** and **Black** young people did not differ from White UK children in referral route, reason for referral or diagnosis.

- **Dual heritage** young people **without a UK parent** differed in referral route and were more likely to self-refer and less likely to be referred by secondary services.

- **White-non-UK** young people were less likely to be referred by secondary services and more likely to be referred by social services. Like non-White minority ethnic groups, they were more likely to be referred for poor parenting.

- **Asian** children were less likely to be given a psychiatric diagnosis as a result of the clinic assessment but more had developmental disorders.

The findings of this study have some similarities and some differences to other similar studies (Kramer *et al.* 2000). For example:

- Unlike the Goodman and Richards (1995) study, this study did not identify a trend for conduct disorders among African Caribbean young people.

- Unlike the findings of Stern *et al.*'s (1990) and Messent and Murrell's (2003) studies, this study did not find comparable diagnostic patterns in Bangladeshi and non-Asian young people.

- Like the Hackett, Hackett and Taylor study (1991), this study found fewer psychiatric diagnoses in the Asian group.

Kramer *et al.* (2000) suggest that such discrepancies between studies may reflect heterogeneity within minority ethnic groups. They further highlight that the absence of the dual heritage category in the Census made it difficult to assess expected rates (based on 1991 Census) and actual rates (study categories) of attendance at the service. This was due to the difficulty in ascertaining how dual heritage individuals classified themselves in the 1991 Census, which did not provide a category for those of dual heritage. The authors suggest that the failure in their study to establish reduced service use by 'Asian' children may be explained by a relative absence of support for these clients from within their own communities. Such a conclusion, however, needs to be regarded in the context of points made earlier (See p.93 – Client perceptions of services).

Jayarajan (2001) also found differences in the ethnic profile of referral to a CAMHS service. 'South Asian' groups were under-represented and African Caribbeans were over-represented, compared to their numbers in the local population. Another important factor was also highlighted by this study, differences in the **linguistic** groups referred:

- English speakers were much more likely to be referred to CAMHS than any other linguistic group. This group was over-represented in an area that is composed predominantly of minority ethnic groups.

- Urdu and Bengali speakers were under-represented.

- Punjabi speakers were closer to the number of referrals expected, given their numbers in the general population.

Primary care

Primary care services play an important role in the early stages of recognising and identifying difficulties. It is suggested that poor recognition of mental health difficulties at the primary care level is an important contributor to fewer young people being referred to CAMHS (Dwivedi 1996). Studies looking at access to mental health services for minority ethnic groups, CAMHS as well as across a broader range of age groups, conclude that the biggest barrier to access is the interface between primary and secondary care (Cohen 2000; Commander *et al.* 1997; Minnis *et al.* in press). Greater attention appears to have been given to the role of GPs than to other primary care staff in available studies. A wide range of agencies and professionals are identified in CAMHS, particularly at Tiers 1 and 2, for whom the recognition of presenting difficulties are relevant.

Commander *et al.* (1997) undertook a study of primary care settings in a culturally diverse inner city area of Birmingham, to look at determinants of access to mental health care in the age range 16–64 years. Commander *et al.* (1997) highlight that one of the main impediments to 'Asians' accessing care occurred at the interface between general practice and specialist services; some people failed to use services at all. The authors suggest that to improve uptake of mental health care, national campaigns should be supplemented by local initiatives targeted at those who are most likely to be unwell but least likely to consult (in their study this was the young, single people and those who were unemployed).

Commander *et al.* (1997) acknowledge the use of crude ethnic categories (Asian, Black and White) but highlight important differences in relation to case recognition for these groups by GPs:

- Mental health problems were found to be more common in the Asian community and they were more likely to consult their GPs compared to Black or White people.

- However, White people were more likely to have their mental health problems identified by their GP than Asian and Black people.

- The most striking feature identified for Black people was the poor level of case recognition in primary care.

- However, there was a marked over-representation of Black people to inpatient facilities.

The findings of this study are consistent with others (Boardman 1987; Cochrane and Sashidharan 1996; Wilson and MacCarthy 1994) that highlight an over-representation of particular minority ethnic groups in specialist services. It is suggested that the failure to identify minority ethnic groups as cases, at an early stage in the development of difficulties, can increase the likelihood of their receiving intervention at the point of crisis.

A study commissioned by the Department of Health (Arber 2000) highlights a range of cultural barriers that relate to clients and the culture of service provision:

- The use of bilingual children as interpreters is highlighted as being of concern, not least because of the possibility of misdiagnosis. In cases of language difference between GP and client, both express a preference for trained health advocates to attend and mediate consultations.

- Cultural differences between GPs and clients who speak the same language can also compromise the quality of consultations.

- Administrative arrangements of GP practices, particularly the appointments system, can be a major barrier to accessing services. 'Walk in' systems were preferred by clients to booked appointment systems.

Child and adolescent mental health services

Similar findings relating to the uptake of services are highlighted in relation to child and adolescent mental health research. Goodman and Richards (1995) found a high rate of more serious diagnoses among African Caribbean children attending child psychiatric clinics. Messent and Murrell (2003) also found that those of African Caribbean origin tended to be referred with more urgent problems and were more likely to be in contact with the service two years later, whereas White British families were least likely to present with urgent problems and least likely to be continuing to be seen.

Kramer *et al.* (2000), however, did not find a trend for more conduct disorders among African Caribbean children, nor did they find less use of psychiatric services by 'Asian' children. The authors again suggest that this discrepancy, as compared to other studies (Commander *et al.* 1997; Stern *et al.* 1990), may be due to heterogeneity in the groups examined and differences in levels of client diversity between different clinics.

Another study looking at under-representation of South Asian (mostly of Pakistani origin) families in a Glasgow CAMHS found fewer referrals of this group by GPs, as compared to their White counterparts (Minnis *et al.* in press). The authors suggest two possibilities to explain this finding:

- South Asian families are less likely to identify unusual behaviour as something that is suitable for medical or therapeutic intervention.

- The difficulties are not being seen as appropriate for referral to CAMHS by the GP. However, having a South Asian GP was not said to improve access to child psychiatric services.

The authors conclude that solutions do not lie simply in raising awareness among clinicians. There are assumptions made by clinicians about family life and help-seeking behaviour that are not necessarily shared by South Asian families. The assumptions inform the structure of assessment, diagnosis and treatment and could become barriers to communication irrespective of there being a common language. Services should seek to understand, rather than change, the culture of minority ethnic groups.

This would support the provision of appropriate services that do not necessarily treat everyone the same but according to individual needs.

Further research

There has been very little research that addresses CAMHS provision for minority ethnic groups in the United Kingdom. Daryanani *et al.* (2001) highlight the need for research in CAMHS with independent samples to:

- analyse relationship between prevalence of child psychiatric disorders in different ethnic groups and referrer bias

- effects of migration and additional socio-economic factors on disproportionate numbers of referrals.

Hardman and Harris (1998) also suggest further research that may be helpful in improving pathways to support.

- Parent conceptualisations of behavioural, emotional and developmental problems in young people and their understanding about the reasons and causes of these.

- Acceptable terminology, for mental health issues, in languages used by local minority ethnic groups.

- Appropriate and effective models of intervention for working with minority ethnic groups, which take into account relevant cultural, social and political issues.

- Communication patterns between GPs and clients and their meaning for both parties.

- Ways of improving the ability of professionals to detect psychological and emotional difficulties in clients.

- Models and explanations used for illness and mental distress by clients from minority ethnic groups.

Information about services

A number of approaches are highlighted in relation to the provision of information. A service may be targeted at a particular community but the needs of individuals within that community must also be taken into account, for example factors related to age or gender (Beliappa 1991;

Bhui *et al.* 1995). This applies to public health campaigns where it is suggested that the health education needs of minority ethnic groups differ and techniques used should be selected to match the context of targeted groups (Bhopal 1991). Health promotion advice has been described as being largely based on knowledge of the ethnic majority (Webb 1996). It is necessary to have knowledge of the social and cultural contexts of communities at whom health promotion initiatives are being targeted and a notion of how the material will be understood.

- Publicity material should be made available in languages relevant to local communities.

- The material should be displayed at relevant community venues such as health centres and community and voluntary organisations.

- Other sources, such as using relevant media (community newspapers and radio stations), should be used.

- Outreach work and link worker posts should be developed.

- Target groups should include local communities as well as relevant other agencies and professionals.

- Information should be provided about how help can be obtained, from where, what services offer and how they can be used appropriately and beneficially.

Box 4.1 Recommendations for publicising services (Hardman and Harris 1998)

The recommendations outlined in Box 4.1 are similar to the views obtained by Messent and Murrell (2003) in relation to suggestions improving access to a CAMHS service. Bhui *et al.* (1995) further suggest that information should be regularly disseminated and include immediate and future planned service developments. Local community groups and representatives of social and religious bodies can be a useful route for conveying information.

FOCUS Survey (Part 2)

Eleven of 14 service managers interviewed said their services did not undertake any targeted publicity although they recognised the need for this to occur.

The need for services to be clear about their ability to respond to an increased access is highlighted by Messent and Murrell (2003) in their study looking at reasons for under-use of CAMHS by the local Bangladeshi community. The feedback obtained from parents, professionals and potential referring agencies in this study indicated that targeted publicity would be likely to increase referrals. However, subsequent discussions in the service generated some concern among staff about the ability of the service to respond to a significant increase in referrals. Success in increasing minority ethnic groups' access runs the risk of becoming a pointless exercise if the ability of the service to respond appropriately to increased demand remains limited.

Flexibility of provision

Flexibility of provision can have an impact on access and refers to a number of aspects such as the time and place where support is provided and the type of intervention offered. Bhui *et al.* (1995) suggest that there should be a range of locally available and flexible treatment packages. The development and provision of such packages should provide opportunities for client involvement. For example, treatment in the home environment may be more culturally familiar than that of inpatient or outpatient facilities and could be provided with the help of family and/or professionals.

Treatment preferences of minority ethnic groups should also be given consideration, however unfamiliar to the professional, with an explicit documented assessment of decision-risk informing the eventual outcome (Carson 1984; Hatcher 1994).

Hardman and Harris (1998) suggest ways in which work can be undertaken in schools and with parents. In relation to schools it is suggested that support could be provided individually or in groups and could be combined with time for socialising or other activities.

- Home visits should be offered where appropriate.

- Support could also be provided through other venues such as health centres and schools.

- Drop-in surgeries should be offered.

- There should be a choice of staff in relation to gender and ethnicity.

In Jayarajan's (2001) study of a CAMHS service, staff noted that not taking into account the religious and cultural beliefs and commitments could result in appointments not being taken up. For example, running clinics on set days and times meant that some Muslim children could not attend because they attended Mosque after school. Similarly, women from some minority groups preferred to be seen at home by a female member of staff; clinic-based appointments and gender of staff could therefore be barriers to access for some clients.

Kramer *et al.* (2000) also noted that there was a low rate of recording of religion. The authors suggest this raises a question about the level of

Recommendations

Each locality develops a directory of all agencies and contact names, who provide culturally sensitive services.

Intake and assessment procedures are reviewed to ensure that they take into account the culturally defined needs of children, adolescents, their families and the community.

Further research is conducted in order to improve the access of children from minority ethnic groups to CAMHS.

Strategies are developed to facilitate partnerships between statutory and voluntary agencies, community groups and individuals from local minority ethnic groups.

significance attributed by clinicians to this variable. Similar conclusions have also been reached by Jayarajan (2001) and Minnis *et al.* (in press).

The delivery of culturally competent services

Delivering culturally appropriate services requires recognition about cultural beliefs and practices at both the practical and therapeutic level. There also needs to be an acknowledgement of the fact that an individual's experience is inextricably linked to their wider social and political context. Consideration also needs to be given to the stage in the migratory process that families have reached as this may have implications for the type of intervention that would be appropriate (Arber 2000; Messent 1992). To become 'culturally competent' services need to extend this awareness into the development of skills, knowledge and policies to deliver effective and appropriate interventions (US Department of Health and Human Services 2001).

FOCUS Survey (Part 2)

When asked if they felt that their service was able to meet the needs of an ethnically and culturally diverse population, 10 out of 14 service managers felt that this was partly achieved.

Cultural competence does more than provide an equal access non-discriminatory service to clients from minority ethnic groups. It involves a broad range of activities which are outlined in Box 4.2.

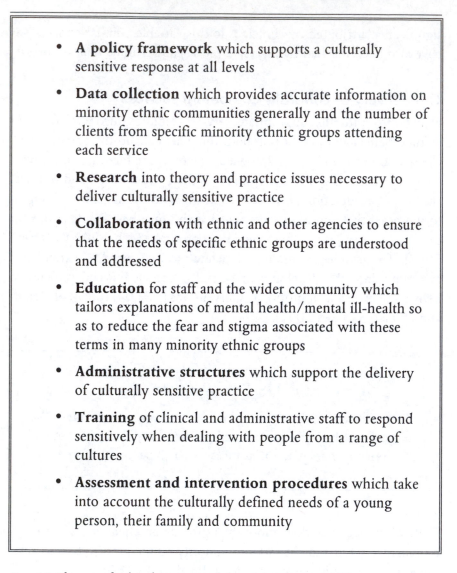

- **A policy framework** which supports a culturally sensitive response at all levels

- **Data collection** which provides accurate information on minority ethnic communities generally and the number of clients from specific minority ethnic groups attending each service

- **Research** into theory and practice issues necessary to deliver culturally sensitive practice

- **Collaboration** with ethnic and other agencies to ensure that the needs of specific ethnic groups are understood and addressed

- **Education** for staff and the wider community which tailors explanations of mental health/mental ill-health so as to reduce the fear and stigma associated with these terms in many minority ethnic groups

- **Administrative structures** which support the delivery of culturally sensitive practice

- **Training** of clinical and administrative staff to respond sensitively when dealing with people from a range of cultures

- **Assessment and intervention procedures** which take into account the culturally defined needs of a young person, their family and community

Box 4.2 Elements of cultural competence (adapted from Luntz 1998)

Planning services

The cultural sensitivity of developing services should be considered throughout the planning and implementation process and *not* as an after-thought whereby the provision of quality services for minority ethnic groups is completed later than all other stages.

FOCUS Survey (Part 2)

Seven of the 14 service managers interviewed said that they did not use data on clients' ethnicity to plan service provision.

There is a lack of knowledge and clarity among service providers as to whether the number of children and adolescents from minority ethnic groups using their service reflects local needs.

Clients from minority ethnic groups did not contribute to the planning of provision in 10 out of the 14 services.

Awareness of professionals about the availability of services

It is suggested that greater awareness among mental health professionals about culturally sensitive services already in existence is necessary (Bhui *et al.* 1995). Each locality should have a register/directory of all agencies and contact persons for all organisations. Such sources would also be invaluable to clients and providers alike who may wish to rapidly identify the most appropriate agencies to deliver interventions as part of a culturally appropriate treatment plan.

Lack of information held by professionals about appropriate provision for minority ethnic groups or the view that certain types of provision will not be appropriate can also affect the pathway to support. For example, Minnis *et al.* (in press) found that some treatment options available outside the CAMHS service were not offered to South Asian families, or were declined by parents; in one case this was said to be recorded as being due to language barriers. It is suggested (Bhui *et al.* 1995) that assessments of individual need may also be hampered by:

1. a lack of known effective interventions

2. unavailability of interventions that minority ethnic groups wish to use

3. absence of appropriate services locally to deliver relevant interventions

4. lack of scientific data to provide a treatment desired by the client.

Each particular cultural group or individual client can place specific demands on service providers, stretching the established and evidence-based range of interventions. These challenges can be addressed through the development of more flexible care packages and a partnership between provider units, minority ethnic group clients and professionals.

Some evidence is emerging from CAMHS that a lack of knowledge about mental health provision among non-health professionals, who may be in a position to refer clients to CAMHS, is significant in fewer referrals being made. For example, Messent and Murrell (2003) in their study looking at reasons for under-referrals to CAMHS found:

- There was a 'remarkable lack of knowledge' about the CAMHS service among local voluntary sector agencies that were providing a service to the Bangladeshi community.

- Staff in these agencies felt that a publicity campaign aimed at them would result in increased number of referrals to CAMHS.

- Clients may have a preference to seek support elsewhere such as through community organisations. These were seen as offering a more holistic service including practical help alongside emotional support. This combination was seen as more likely to attract Bangladeshi clients.

- CAMHS workers doing outreach work within the community were seen as potentially useful as a bridging tool.

FOCUS Survey (Part 2)

Of the 14 managers all except two service managers said that their services liaised with other agencies who had relevant expertise in addressing the needs of minority ethnic groups. The nature of contact varies; some is client-focused (e.g. outreach work) and other is more service-focused (e.g. joint training).

Reflecting cultural diversity in services

Accessibility of services by minority ethnic groups could be enhanced by making the environments of services more culturally sensitive so that they reflect the ethnic diversity of the local population, for example, through the use of positive visual images and provision of signs and literature in relevant languages that reflect the ethnicity of the local community (Webb-Johnson 1991).

The quality of client and staff interactions can be important contributing factors to the underutilisation of psychiatric facilities (Brewin 1980). Staff, in this respect, includes employees at all levels from administrative to clinical personnel. Bhui *et al.* (1995) suggest that health care workers, including psychiatrists, irrespective of their own cultural background, should be involved in some sessional time devoted to organisations led by minority ethnic groups. This could be achieved through encouraging cross-cultural psychiatry training placements to facilitate staff to gain experience of working in culturally diverse contexts. It is further suggested that the presence or absence of such posts could act as a measure of the cultural sensitivity of services. Other measures of cultural competence could include employment of bilingual staff, a clear strategy to involve advocates from minority ethnic groups and targets for specified service improvements that are annually reviewed.

Addressing client and professional differences

Anane-Agyei *et al.* (2002) demonstrate an approach adopted by the African Families Project which was set up following the observed unhealthy dynamic between clients and professionals. The initiative works with a range of professionals from health, social services and education sectors and highlights the following features:

- The project attempts to maintain a balance of staff ensuring there were African as well as White workers in order that both traditions and ways of seeing can be represented.

- In order to address the assumed mistrust and apprehension of parents that agencies judge them negatively, staff make efforts on first contact to communicate respect for parents' good intentions for their children.

- Follow-up interviews with parents, conducted by independent staff, have highlighted their appreciation of these efforts.

- These interviews also revealed that parents valued the presence of African staff whom they saw as ensuring their values and ways of doing things would not be misinterpreted.

- Statutory responsibilities of professionals, legal requirements and other information is communicated in a manner that conveys respect for parents as being essentially caring. In order to avoid the possibility of parents feeling their authority is being undermined, the initial contact is organised to take place without the children being present.

Krause and Miller (1995) point out the need to guard against overemphasis on the need for professionals to have information about their clients' ethnic groups and cultures. Relevant information has its place but can lead to drawbacks if:

- Issues relating to professionals receive less attention.

- The status of available information is not clear; in the absence of an indication about how the information was acquired there is a danger of stereotyping.

- There is no definition given to words such as 'ethnicity' or 'culture'. In the absence of clarity regarding key words and terms, it can be difficult to question assumptions.

The need to guard against assuming that available information can be used by clinicians to help clients is also highlighted. Such an assumption could lead to issues about inequalities in power, between clinician and client, not being addressed. It is necessary to acknowledge that clinicians cannot be experts on how people from different cultural backgrounds think and feel. This is not least because culture is not a uniform concept and clients who identify with a particular culture may nevertheless have varying affiliation to the values and ideas associated with that culture. Furthermore, cultural meanings can be reinterpreted and redefined through interaction with others (Boyd-Franklin 1989). Assuming cultural uniformity could lead to discriminatory service delivery if the emphasis on culture leads to consideration for basic and general human needs being given secondary importance (Montalvo and Gutierrez 1988). Maitra (1996) discusses the difficulties with universal assumptions (about 'human' values), and the complex relationships between professional expertise, ethnic matching and cultural knowledge.

Feedback received by FOCUS from the voluntary sector to inform this report indicated that the linguistic and ethnic profile of the staff group can be an important influence on the profile of the client group. A culturally and linguistically diverse staff group may achieve similar diversity in client groups. However, the notion that needs of clients from minority ethnic groups are best addressed by professionals who share the same ethnicity is increasingly questioned (Krause and Miller 1995; Minnis *et al.* in press). An important distinction is between employing staff from minority ethnic groups as part of an overall equal opportunities policy and good practice, and passing over to them the bulk of responsibility in addressing the needs of minority ethnic groups. The latter is unacceptable for a number of reasons. For example:

- While some clients may wish to see a professional from the same ethnic background as themselves, others may not. This also applies to other characteristics such as gender of professionals (Fatemilehin and Coleman 1999; Hardman and Harris 1998).

- Responsibility for meeting the needs of minority ethnic groups should be shared by all staff and at all levels of the service (Krause and Miller 1995).

- It should not be assumed that fewer problems are likely to arise between client and clinician if they are from the same ethnic group (Cohen 2000; Minnis *et al.* in press).

- A shared cultural affiliation between individuals does not mean they also share exactly the same norms, values, beliefs and practices. Consideration needs to be given to general human issues alongside cultural ones (Boyd-Franklin 1989; Montalvo and Gutierrez 1988).

Language and communication

Language and communication are important, not only in the initial stages of recognising difficulties and accessing support, but also in the provision of clinical support and other interventions. Overcoming barriers presented by differences in language between client and professional requires careful consideration as does the use of translation and interpreting services. Certain expressions of psychological distress are culturally and linguistically specific and their meaning could be lost in translation (Ananthanarayanan 1994; Cochrane and Sashidharan 1996). This applies not only to verbal translations but also to tools such as rating scales and screening questionnaires that have been standardised and validated on the White population and often in the US but not the UK.

INTERPRETERS

A number of CAMHS-focused studies highlight issues relating to the use of interpreters. Clinicians in Jayarajan's (2001) study of a CAMHS in Birmingham reported a number of difficulties in the use of interpreters:

- **Confidentiality** – Where interpreters were recruited from the same community as the client or were otherwise known to them, either the clients expressed concern that information would not remain confidential or clinicians felt that clients were not disclosing relevant information.

- **Personal details of interpreter** – Factors such as the interpreter's age, gender, faith and caste were said to have a significant effect on the dynamics with the family and as such could influence the clinical process.

- **Skill of the interpreter** – Staff reported they were frequently only hearing part of the story and felt it would be beneficial to be involved in training interpreters on CAMHS issues.

The need to consider the possibility that a greater amount of time may be needed when working with families when clinician and client do not share a first language, whether or not working through an interpreter, is highlighted.

Minnis *et al.* (in press) also highlight a number of difficulties encountered by clinicians at a CAMHS in Glasgow. Language was said to be a major barrier in assessment, and language mismatch between family members and clinician was mentioned in 35 per cent of cases. Having a different interpreter attend each session was said to make it difficult to establish a working relationship with the family. Success in the use of interpreters was rare and important family members were excluded from the process because of language mismatch. Even if parents attended sessions they did not always participate if there was no common language with the clinician. Involving, or attempts made to involve, interpreters were not always recorded in case notes, suggesting the approach of mental health disciplines may not give sufficient emphasis to language and communication issues.

The choice of treatment offered to minority ethnic groups was said to be limited in this study and in some cases inappropriate. Treatment was said to be affected by difficulties encountered in assessment and by language mismatch. This resulted in at least one child receiving drug treatment without a satisfactory assessment and four families not being offered treatment that would have been offered to their majority (White) counterparts experiencing the same difficulties. The authors suggest this is a clear indication of inequities in service delivery.

Communication difficulties were experienced at the level of **shared language** and the **conceptual level**. For example, if parent and clinician shared a common language this did not necessarily mean that they also shared notions of 'normal' in relation to family life, gender roles, parenting and so on.

Addressing client need through an interpreter requires three sets of dyadic relationships to be negotiated. The interpreter is the key channel for communication between client and therapist (Faust and Drickey 1986). Different expectations placed on interpreters by the therapist and the client can make it difficult to reach clarity of the interpreter's role. A further complication can be presented if the overall service also lacks clarity about the role of interpreters, resulting in the possibility of their taking on several roles such as (Meyers 1992; Raval 1996):

- **straightforward interpreting**

- **community work** – providing interpreting from within the community

- **link work** – in addition to interpreting, also identifying and understanding the needs of the client and supporting them to make informed choices about services

- **advocate** – for the client

- **cultural broker** – acting as cultural consultant for the service and giving meaning to client responses as well as being the channel for communication.

The lack of a distinct professional status for interpreters raises issues about power and professional boundaries. The need for consideration about the professional status of interpreters, organisational representation and a higher profile within the service is highlighted (Tribe 1991).

The need to guard against treating interpreters as cultural experts is also highlighted (Messent 2003; Raval 1996). A more realistic approach would be to see their perspective as one of a number of possibilities that may be useful in therapy.

Working with an interpreter may require some modification to standard approaches of delivering interventions (Kline *et al.* 1980; Roy 1992). The need for more sessional time for interventions is suggested, even if there is a shared language but cultural differences exist between client and clinician because:

- Communication may be slower.

- There may be a loss of verbal and non-verbal cues.

- There may be greater detachment between client and therapist.

A lack of continuity in the use of interpreters (frequent use of different interpreters) is unlikely to facilitate a good working relationship between therapist and interpreter and is likely to have an unhelpful impact on any ongoing work with clients. A further consideration relates to the emotional impact on interpreters of working in mental health settings.

Services need to avoid seeing training in the use of interpreting as a one-way process, that it is interpreters who have to acquire the skills to work with other staff and not vice versa. Joint training is more likely to ensure that the collaborative nature of interpreting remains prominent and due consideration is given to the complexity and value of both clinician's and interpreter's roles (Krause and Miller 1995; Messent 2003; Westermeyer 1991).

A significant point is made by Pearce (1989) who highlights that working with interpreters is essentially not that different to good practice in working with clients who share the same language. Major differences can exist in world views between people who share the same language. However, it is far more likely that a client who speaks a different language will be asked to clarify what they mean by certain words and phrases than a client with whom a common language is shared, though the differences may be just as great with the latter.

A linguistic group whose needs often go unrecognised is the African Caribbean community, due the assumption that they speak English (Fatemilehin and Coleman 1999). Many African Caribbean families speak patois as their first language and there can be a tendency to overlook the possible implications this may have on the expression of mental distress and subsequent access to relevant support.

A guide to using professional interpreters in health services is available online: www.vtpu.org.au/programs/servicedev/service.html.

There is a continuing debate as to whether mental health services for minority ethnic groups should be delivered through mainstream services or through culture-matched facilities (Flaskerud 1986). It is probably not

Recommendations

Intake and assessment procedures need to be reviewed to ensure that they take into account the culturally defined needs of children, adolescents, their families and the community.

Services need to review the provision and training of interpreters to ensure that best practice is achieved.

a case of either/or but rather that both need to be provided. Mainstream services need to make greater efforts to improve their cultural competence as well as improve their links with specialist facilities for minority ethnic groups.

Staff training/competency

It is suggested that better training is needed for all professionals linked to mental health in order to improve the assessment and diagnosis of mental health difficulties in minority ethnic groups (Fernando 1988). For example, though psychiatrists, police and approved social workers have responsibilities to recognise mental health problems under the 1983 Mental Health Act, only approved social workers have a statutory requirement to show an understanding of working in a multi-ethnic society (MIND 2001). The Reed Report (1990) highlights the conclusion of the Mental Health Act Commission that many professionals had insufficient awareness about the different needs of minority ethnic communities; there appeared to be limited understanding of institutional racism and the effect of cultural differences on the nature of mental health. In such circumstances the accuracy of diagnosis is seen as questionable.

The failure to identify cases highlights the need for improved training and this should pay attention to local factors influencing detection (Commander *et al.* 1997).

Webb-Johnson (1991) highlights some elements that could be included in training programmes for professionals. These are suggested for staff from across disciplines and at different levels of provision from primary to more specialist interventions. In CAMHS this would include staff located in the four tiers. The following elements of training are considered relevant to the recognition of minority ethnic group needs:

- the impact of socio-economic and political factors on minority ethnic groups

- effects of racism and discrimination on mental health

- highlighting and challenging assumptions and stereotypes based on Eurocentric norms

- attitudes to and experiences of distress and illness among minority ethnic groups from local communities

- ways of coping in different local communities such as through prayer or traditional healers

- verbal and non-verbal communication and use of interpreters, including barriers to effective communication and possible consequences

- the importance of empowering communities through initiatives such as awareness-raising.

FOCUS Survey (Part 2)

Only two service managers of the 14 interviewed said that staff received *regular* training to meet the needs of an ethnically diverse client group.

Twelve of the 14 teams did not undertake a formal evaluation after the training was provided.

Twelve of the 14 service managers felt that staff would benefit from additional training in this area.

'Good enough understanding' is described by Krause and Miller (1995) as that which provides a sufficient starting point to enable clients to react, respond and feel encouraged. It does not require therapists to see things exclusively from the client's point of view.

There is a clear need for cultural competence in training for all mental health disciplines. Factors such as a lack of knowledge about the client's culture, lack of relevant clinical training, difference in cultural values and beliefs between clinician and client may make it difficult to provide appropriate interventions (Bhui *et al.* 1995; Boyd-Franklin 1989; Hardy and Laszloffy 1995; Miller and Thomas 1994). For CAMHS staff consideration needs to be given to the integration of cultural knowledge into a developmental framework. This would involve consultation with members of minority ethnic groups to understand cultural variables in growth, development and bonding which exist in different ethnic groups (Cross, Bazron, Dennis, Isaacs 1989).

Balancing cultural awareness and cultural sensitivity

An important distinction is highlighted in relation to cultural competence, that between **cultural awareness** and **cultural sensitivity** (Hardy and Laszloffy 1995; Miller and Thomas 1994; Patel 2000):

- Cultural awareness refers to knowledge about various cultures.

- Cultural sensitivity refers to experiences that challenge individuals to explore their personal cultural issues.

There can be a tendency to view cultural competence in relation to **awareness** and neglect **sensitivity**. This imbalance, the over-emphasis on characteristics of cultural groups, can result in little or no attention being paid to how professionals' own cultural identities influence understanding and acceptance of those who are culturally similar and dissimilar.

Five key components have been identified (Kim 1995) as being fundamental to practising in a culturally sensitive way:

- awareness and acceptance of cultural differences

- capacity for cultural self-awareness

- understanding the dynamics of difference

- becoming as knowledgeable as possible about the culture of individual clients

- adapting practice skills to fit the cultural context of the patient and family.

As discussed in Chapter 2, much of our current knowledge of child development and normal and abnormal behaviour is based on Western concepts. Clinicians need to consider the value and use of accepted therapeutic interventions and how they may need to be adapted when working with children and adolescents and their families from minority ethnic groups.

The teaching of cultural competence should also consider the perspective from which trainers *actually* teach and how they are *perceived* to teach (Miller and Thomas 1994). Furthermore, cultural competence needs to be seen as a core component of training which, in addition to allocating specific time to this issue, also ensures that it informs all other areas of training. The essence of the Race Relations Amendment Act 2000 is in fact to ensure that considerations about cultural issues are built into all aspects of mainstream policy, planning and provision.

Recommendations

Training in cultural competence is incorporated into the personal development plans of clinicians and administrative staff. This training should include:

- general principles of cultural sensitivity

- the complexity of culturally sensitive therapeutic interventions and possible approaches that can be implemented

- ways of involving the wider community such as religious leaders, community leaders or the extended family

- good practice when working with interpreters.

Evaluation

Evaluating the impact of service provision is an important component of service delivery as is client involvement in this process. This applies to the effectiveness of interventions for individual clients as well as the delivery of the overall service. Bhui *et al.* (1995) also highlight the need for evaluation of new health and social care policies on minority ethnic groups. Health service restructuring should routinely evaluate the impact of new models of service delivery on minority ethnic groups, not least because for people already alienated to existing services, new developments in services not evaluated can result in further disadvantage. Access to appropriate support can be a complex process, which can be further exacerbated if language and customs inhibit the successful completion of forms and other criteria required by services. Services should evaluate the progress made by people from minority ethnic groups in negotiating institutionalised barriers.

FOCUS Survey (Part 2)

Nine of the 14 service managers said that their service did not evaluate the impact of service provision for minority ethnic groups.

Recommendations

Services are developed and evaluated in collaboration with members of minority ethnic groups.

Conclusions

In order to meet the mental health needs of children and adolescents from minority ethnic groups, commissioners and service providers need to review a wide range of issues. Consideration needs to be given to user involvement in the broadest sense, to the flexible provision of services, and to training and support for staff.

Commissioners have a key role in defining need and setting standards for the provision of services and this role is not currently being fulfilled. The commitment of the Government to involving patients and users is particularly relevant to this client group. The need to actively inform minority ethnic groups and seek their involvement in planning and evaluating care cannot be overstated.

Mental health professionals need to increase their awareness of individuals and their cultural context in order to deliver appropriate care. Services need to actively target minority ethnic groups in order to ensure that they are aware of the availability of services that will be equipped to meet their needs.

More carefully designed research is needed to examine the pathways and barriers to care for particular minority ethnic groups.

It should be acknowledged that providing appropriate care for children and adolescents from minority ethnic groups cannot be fully achieved without additional resources. Training staff, providing and training interpreters, and the additional time required to provide treatment using interpreters all have important resource implications.

References

Anane-Agyei, A., Lobatto, W. and Messent, P. (2002) 'The African Families Project: A Black and White Issue.' In B. Mason and A. Sawyerr (eds) *Exploring the unsaid: creativity, risks and dilemmas in working cross culturally.* London: Karnac.

Ananthanarayanan, T.S. (1994) 'Epidemiology of mental illness among Asians in the UK.' *British Journal of Hospital Medicine 52*, 500–506.

Arber, S. (2000) *Primary Health Care Services for Children from Minority Ethnic Groups.* London: Department of Health.

Bahl, V. (1998) 'Ethnic minority groups: national perspective.' In S. Rawaf and V. Bahl (eds) *Assessing health needs of people from minority ethnic groups* pp.3–21. London: Royal College of Physicians.

Beliappa, J. (1991) *Illness or Distress – Alternative Models of Mental Health.* London: Confederation of Indian Organisations (UK).

Bhopal, R. (1991) 'Health Education and Ethnic Minorities.' *British Medical Journal 302*, 1, 1338.

Bhugra, D. and Cochrane, R. (1997) 'Incidence and Outcomes of Schizophrenia in Whites, African-Caribbeans and Asians in London.' *Psychological Medicine 27*, 791–798

Bhui, K., Christie, Y. and Bhugra, D. (1995) 'The essential elements of culturally sensitive psychiatric services.' *International Journal of Social Psychiatry 41*, 242–256.

Boardman, A. (1987) 'The General Health Questionnaire and the detection of emotional disorder by General Practitioners.' *British Journal of Psychiatry 151*, 373–381.

Bourne, H. (1990) 'Letter to the Editor.' *British Medical Journal 301*, 240.

Boyd-Franklin, N. (1989) *Black families in Therapy: A Multisystems Approach.* New York: Guildford University Press.

Brewin, C. (1980) 'Explaining the Lower Rates of Psychiatric Treatment Among Asian Immigrants to the United Kingdom: A Preliminary Study.' *Social Psychiatry 15*, 17–19.

Bhugra, D. (1996) 'Setting up services for ethnic minorities.' In M. Weller and M. Muijen (eds) *Dimensions of Community Mental Health Care.* London: Saunders.

Carson, D. (1984) *Risk Taking with Mentally Disordered Offenders.* Southampton: SLE Publications.

Chandra, J. (1996) *Facing up to difference: a toolkit for creating culturally competent health services for black and minority ethnic communities.* London: King's Fund.

Cochrane, R. and Sashidharan, S. (1996) 'The mental health needs of ethnic minorities.' In W. Ahmed and T. Sheldon (eds) *The Mental Health Needs of Ethnic Minorities* pp.105–126. York: University of York.

Cohen, S. (2000) *Executive Summary: Primary Health Care Services for Children from Ethnic Minority Groups.* London: Department of Health.

Commander, M.J. Sashidharan, S.P., Odell, S. and Surtees, P.G. (1997) 'Access to mental health care in an inner city health district II: association with demographic factors.' *British Journal of Psychiatry 170,* 317–320.

Cross, T., Bazron, B., Dennis, K.W. and Isaacs, M. (1989) *Towards a culturally competent system of care: a monograph on effective service for minority children who are severely emotionally disturbed, volume 1.* Georgetown, University of Child Development Centre. Washington DC: CASSP Technical Assistance Center.

Daryanani, R., Hindley, P., Evans, C., Fahy, P. and Turk, J. (2001) 'Ethnicity and Use of a Child and Adolescent Mental Health Service.' *Child Psychology and Psychiatry Review 6,* 127–132.

Dwivedi, K. (1996) 'Introduction.' In K. Dwivedi and V. Varma (eds) *Meeting the needs of ethnic minority children: A handbook for professionals* pp.1–16. London: Jessica Kingsley Publishers.

Fatemilehin, I.A. and Coleman, P.G. (1999) 'You've got to have a Chinese chef to cook Chinese food!! Issues of power and control in the provision of mental health services.' *Journal of Community and Applied Social Psychology 9,* 101–117.

Faust, S. and Drickey, R. (1986) 'Working with Interpreters.' *Journal of Family Practice 22,* 131–138.

Fenton, S. and Sadiq-Sangster, A. (1996) 'Culture, relativism and the expression of mental distress.' *Sociology of Health and Illness 18,* 66–85.

Fernando, S. (1988) *Race and Culture in Psychiatry.* London: Tavistock/Routledge.

Flaskerud, J.H. (1986) 'The effects of culture-compatible intervention on the utilization of mental health services by minority clients.' *Community Mental Health Journal 22,* 2, 127–141.

Goldberg, D. and Hodes, M. (1992) 'The poison of racism and the self poisoning of adolescents.' *Journal of Family Therapy 14,* 51–67.

Goldberg, D. and Huxley, P. (1980) *Mental Illness in the Community: The Pathway to Psychiatric Care.* London: Tavistock.

Goodman, R. and Richards, H. (1995) 'Child and adolescent psychiatric presentations of second generation Afro-Caribbeans in Britain.' *British Journal of Psychiatry 167*, 362–369.

Green, G., Bradby, H., Chan, A., Lee, M. and Eldridge, K. (2002) 'Is the English NHS meeting the needs of mentally distressed Chinese women?' *Journal of Health Services Research and Policy 7*, 4, 216–221.

Hackett, L. and Hackett, R. (1993) 'Parental ideas of normal and deviant behaviour.' *British Journal of Psychiatry 162*, 353–357.

Hackett, R., Hackett, L. and Taylor, D. C. (1991) 'Psychological disturbance and its associations in the children of the Gujerati community.' *Journal of Psychology and Psychiatry 32*, 851–856.

Hardman, E. and Harris, R. (1998) *Developing and evaluating community mental health services: Volume 1, The Bangladeshi community, assessment of need.* London: Tavistock Clinic.

Hardy, K. V. and Laszloffy, T. A. (1995) 'The Cultural Genogram: Key to training culturally competent family therapists.' *Journal of Marital and Family Therapy 21*, 227–237.

Hatcher, S. (1994) 'Decision analysis in psychiatry.' *British Journal of Psychiatry 166*, 184–190.

Health Advisory Service (1995) *Child and Adolescent Mental Health Services: Together We Stand.* London: HMSO.

House of Commons Health Committee (1997) *Child and Adolescent Mental Health Services. Health Committee Fourth Report: Session 1996–97, HC 26-I.* London: HMSO.

Jayarajan, U. (2001) *The Demographic Profile of the Children and Young People Referred to and Seen by Birmingham CAMHS.* Birmingham Children's Hospital NHS Trust.

Kim, W.J. (1995) 'A training guideline of cultural competence for child and adolescent psychiatric residencies.' *Child Psychiatry and Human Development 26*, 125–136.

Kline, F., Acosta, F., Austin, W., Johnson, R.G. Jr. (1980) 'The misunderstood Spanish speaking patient.' *American Journal of Psychiatry 137*, 1530–1533.

Knight, B. (1993) *Voluntary Action.* London: Home Office.

Kramer, T., Evans, N. and Garralda, M.E. (2000) 'Ethnic diversity among child and adolescent psychiatric attenders.' *Child Psychology and Psychiatry 5*, 169–175.

Krause, I.B. and Miller, A. (1995) 'Culture and family therapy.' In S. Fernando (ed) *Mental Health in a Multi-Ethnic Society: A Multi-Disciplinary Handbook.* pp.149–171. London: Routledge.

Kurtz, Z., Thornes, R. and Wolkind, S. (1994) *Services for the mental health of children and young people in England: A national review.* London: South West Thames Regional Health Authority and Department of Health.

Kurtz, Z. (1996) *Treating Children Well: A guide to the evidence base in commissioning and managing services for the mental health of children and young people.* London: Mental Health Foundation.

Leff, J. (1981) *Psychiatry Around the Globe: A Transcultural View.* New York: Dekker.

Littlewood, R. and Lipsedge, M. (1997) *Aliens and Alienist: Ethnic Minorities and Psychiatry* (3rd edition). London: Routledge.

Luntz, J. (1998) *Cultural Competence in CAMHS: Report on the usage of child and adolescent mental health services by NESB adolescents and their families.* Australian Transcultural Mental Health Network, University of Melbourne: Australia.

Maitra, B. (1996) 'Child abuse: A universal 'diagnostic' category? The implication of culture in definition and assessment.' *International Journal of Social Psychiatry 42,* 4, 287–304.

Messent, P. (1992) 'Working with Bangladeshi Families in the East End of London.' *Journal of Family Therapy 14,* 287–304.

Messant, P. (2003) 'From postmen to makers of meaning: a model for collaborative work between clinicians and interpreters.' In R. Tribe and H. Raval (eds) *Working with Interpreters in Mental Health.* Hove: Brunner-Routledge.

Messent, P. and Murrell, M. (2003) 'Research leading to action: A study of accessibility of a CAMH Service to ethnic minority families.' *Child and Adolescent Mental Health 8,* 3, 118–124.

Meyers, C. (1992) 'Among children and their families: Consideration of cultural influences in assessment.' *The American Journal of Occupational Therapy 46,* 737–744.

Miller, A. and Thomas, L. (1994) 'Ethnicity, Culture, Race and Family Therapy.' *Context 20.*

MIND (2001) *Factsheets: The Mental Health of the South Asian Community in Britain.* London: MIND Publications.

Minnis, H., Kelly, E. and Bradby, H. (in press) *The Use of Child Psychiatry by South Asian Families in South Glasgow.*

Montalvo, B. and Gutierrez, G. (1988) 'The development of cultural identity: A developmental-ecological constraint.' In C. Falicov (ed) *Family Transitions: Continuity and change over the life cycle.* New York: Guilford.

Mumford, D. (1994) 'Transcultural aspects of rehabilitation.' In C. Hume and I. Pullen (eds) *Rehabilitation for mental health problems.* London: Churchill Livingstone.

Nadirshaw, Z. (1993) 'Therapeutic Practice in Multiracial Britain.' *Transcultural Psychiatry (UK) Bulletin 1,* 1–4.

O'Brian, C. (1990) 'Family therapy with Black families.' *Journal of Family Therapy 12,* 3–16.

Office for Public Management (1996) *Responding to Diversity: A Study of Commissioning Issues and Good Practice in Purchasing Minority Ethnic Health.* London: Office for Public Management.

Patel, N. (ed) (2000) *Clinical Psychology: 'Race' and culture: A Training Manual.* London: BPS Books.

Pearce, W. (1989) *Communication and the Human Condition.* Carbondale, Il: Southern Illinois University Press.

Raval, H. (1996) 'A systemic perspective on working with interpreters.' *Clinical Child Psychology and Psychiatry 1*, 29–43.

Rawaf, S. (1998) 'Theoretical Framework.' In S. Rawaf and V. Bahl (eds) *Assessing health needs of people from minority ethnic groups* pp.21–35. London: Royal College of Physicians.

Reed Report (1990) *Race, Gender and Equal Opportunities.* London: HMSO.

Roy, C. (1992) 'A sociolinguistic analysis of the interpreter's role.' *Sign Language Studies 5*, 21–61.

Secretary of State for Health (1997) *The New NHS: Modern, Dependable.* London: Stationary Office.

Singh, J. (1998) *Developing the role of the black and minority ethnic voluntary sector in a changing NHS.* London: Department of Health.

Stern, G., Cottrell, D. and Holmes, J. (1990) 'Patterns of attendance of child psychiatry outpatients with special reference to Asian families.' *British Journal of Psychiatry 156*, 384–387.

Tribe, R. (1991) 'Bi-Cultural Workers. Bridging the Gap or Damming the Flow. Paper presented in Chile.' In H. Rawal and R. Tribe (eds) *Working with interpreters in mental health.* London: Routledge.

US Department of Health and Human Services (2001) *Mental Health: Culture, Race and Ethnicity – A supplement to mental health: A Report of the Surgeon General.* Rockville, MD: US Department of Health and Human Services, Substance Abuse and Mental Health Services.

Webb, E. (1996) 'Meeting the needs of minority ethnic communities.' *Archives of disease in childhood 74*, 264–267.

Webb-Johnson, A. (1991) *A Cry for Change.* Condeferation of Indian Organisations, London: Russell Press Ltd.

Webb-Johnson, A. and Nadirshaw, Z. (1993) 'Good Practice in Transcultural Psychotherapy: An Asian Perspective.' Presented at a symposium BJGC 21st January.

Westermeyer, J. (1991) 'Working with an interpreter in psychiatric assessments.' *Journal of Nervous and Mental Disease 178*, 745.

Wilson, M. and MacCarthy, B. (1994) 'GP consultation as a factor in the low rate of mental health service use among Asians.' *Psychological Medicine 24*, 113–119.

5 Refugee Children in the UK

Matthew Hodes

Definitions: Who are refugees?

Over the last century persecution, war and organised violence have led to the movement of large populations (Kushner and Knox 1999; UNHCR 2000). Many people are internally displaced within their own country, but others flee across international borders and seek asylum in other countries. In the UK, a refugee is a person whose application for asylum has been accepted by the Home Office. An asylum applicant is granted refugee status if that person meets the criteria laid down in the 1951 United Nations Convention on Refugees. The UN defines a refugee as someone who:

> Owing to well-founded fear of being persecuted for reasons of race, religion, nationality, membership of a particular social group or political opinion, is outside the country of his nationality and is unable or, owing to such fear, is unwilling to avail himself of the protection of that country; or who, not having a nationality and being outside that country of his former habitual residence as a result of such events, is unable or, owing to such fear, is unwilling to return to it.

Within the UK, when the Home Office thinks that the applicant does not reach these criteria, but that it would be dangerous for them to return to their country, humanitarian or discretionary leave may be granted (previously known as exceptional leave to remain (ELR)).

The centrally administered asylum support scheme in the UK is the National Asylum Support Service (NASS), which was established by the Immigration and Asylum Act 1999. NASS is responsible for the organisation of asylum seekers' applications and services. Asylum seekers, including adults with children, may be required to stay in induction centres (located near ports of entry such as Heathrow Airport) for screening and identification, then moved to accommodation centres until their applications have been processed. They may then be dispersed across the UK. Asylum seekers are unable to work or obtain permanent local authority housing.

Unaccompanied asylum-seeking children under 18 years of age are supported by local authority services, not NASS. These children are not dispersed. Unaccompanied children who are 'looked after' (Section 20 of the Children Act 1989) are entitled to the full range of service from the local authority social service departments including leaving care support. However, many unaccompanied children, especially those aged 16–17 years, are not 'looked after' but recognised to be children in need and are supported under Section 17 of the Children Act 1989. They may reside in foster families, children's homes or homeless accommodation. All refugee and asylum-seeking children can use pre-school facilities and children aged 5–16 years are required to go to school.

People with humanitarian or discretionary leave are entitled to work and obtain local authority benefits such as housing. In these respects, they are similar to those with refugee status. However, humanitarian or discretionary leave are not permanent status and application must be made to obtain refugee status after three years which is usually granted.

How many refugees are there?

According to data compiled by the United Nations High Commission for Refugees (UNHCR), at the end of 2000 there were over 21 million people of concern, of whom just over 12 million were refugees and 5 million were internally displaced. Until the 1990s most of this population were living in the Middle East and Africa. The Yugoslavian tragedy and other conflicts in Eastern Europe have resulted in larger numbers of refugees in Europe. Currently there are over 7 million refugees, asylum seekers and internally displaced people in Europe.

The UK has received 454,445 applications for asylum over the past 16 years, rising from 4389 in 1985 to 80,315 in 2000 (Refugee Council 2002). Approximately 40 per cent of these applications are successful. These asylum seekers and refugees coming to the UK have come from many countries but especially Sri Lanka, Iraq, Iran and the Horn of Africa, and recently many from former Yugoslavia and the USSR, Afghanistan and China.

For many years there have been thousands of unaccompanied children seeking asylum in the UK. In 2000 the Home Office received 2733 asylum applications from children and the most frequent country of origin was former Yugoslavia (24 per cent). A survey carried out in England in 2001 identified over 6000 unaccompanied asylum seekers supported by local authorities; most were living in London or Kent (Refugee Council 2001).

The experiences of asylum seekers and refugees

Asylum seekers and refugees travel to the UK because of exposure to, or fear of, organised violence and war, and forcible displacement. The actual exposure of the children of asylum seekers to war and organised violence is very variable. At one extreme are youngsters who survived massive genocide, detention and abuse of the kind that affected large parts of their countries such as Cambodia under the Khymer Rouge in the 1970s or in Rwanda in 1994. Other youngsters have been exposed to genocide or war that affected their communities or families, such as that of the Kurds in Iraq or in the Yugoslavian wars in Bosnia in 1992–6, and the Albanian Kosovars in the war in 1998–9. Some asylum-seeking or refugee children had less direct exposure but an awareness of war, perhaps from family discussions, media reports or seeing warplanes flying overhead. Some refugee children, offspring of asylum seekers, were born in the UK or other resettlement countries, and will have not been exposed to the adversities described above.

Within a family, exposure to war and losses may vary between family members. Fathers are especially likely to have been detained, tortured and killed (Gorst-Unsworth and Goldenberg 1998; Montgomery 1998), although children may be detained and imprisoned. However, women may also have been detained and may have been exposed to specific forms of maltreatment such as sexual abuse and rape. Unaccompanied children may have experienced a higher level of exposure to war and violence and experienced many losses, such as separations from and deaths of parents, older siblings and other relatives.

The journey to safe countries may be very arduous. Families may have to travel via intermediate countries and sometimes risk detention and privation en route. Upon arrival there will still be many stresses such as detention, high levels of mobility, and racial harassment. Families may experience financial hardship, as parents may be unable to work. Uncertainties may last for many months or years regarding asylum applications. Barriers to services may exist because of language, and it may be difficult to access health care and even obtain school places (Aldous, Bardsley, Daniell, Gair, Jacobson, Lowdell, Morgan, Storkey and Taylor 1999).

Refugees have had experiences that show some similarities and differences with those of economic immigrants (Hodes 2000). Both groups may experience discrimination and exclusion, poverty and social isolation on arrival in the UK. For children there may be bullying at school or other forms of harassment. Both economic immigrants and refugees experience the loss of their countries of origin and find it hard to adapt to new ways of living. Children who go to school may learn English more rapidly than their parents, and acquire English or cosmopolitan values and a culturally mixed peer group. The different generations may assimilate at different rates over time and this may set up tensions and intra-familial conflict.

A number of experiences distinguish refugees from economic migrants. Economic immigrants may have planned their destination and journey, and will be able to maintain links with their relatives and communities in their countries of origin and make return visits. By contrast refugees frequently have had no, or very limited, opportunity to plan their flight. They may be leaving communities and societies that have been destroyed by organised violence or the threat of it. There may be further hardships on arrival for the asylum seekers, such as detention and dispersal, which may increase social isolation, economic hardship and unemployment (Hodes and Goldberg 2002).

Implications for mental health

The reasons why people become asylum seekers and refugees are also experiences that cause high levels of psychological distress and increase risk for psychiatric disorder (Hodes 2000; Rousseau 1995; Sack 1998). A number of important issues arise.

1. Can psychiatric disorders be recognised in refugees?

There is evidence that the existing psychiatric classificatory systems are valid cross-culturally (Hodes 2002a; Sack 1998). Specifically, psychiatric disorders that frequently occur in refugees such as post-traumatic stress disorder, depression and adjustment disorders can be recognised in young people from diverse cultures. The psychiatric classificatory systems are multiaxial, and have a psychosocial axis which codes many social adversities including disrupted child rearing and migration (WHO 1992, 1996). This issue has become controversial because of claims that cultural differences and the experiences of loss of refugees mean that existing psychiatric classificatory systems are too narrow and that epidemiological comparisons are not meaningful (Eisenbruch 1991; Summerfield 2000a, 2000b). This controversy is less relevant in contexts such as community child mental health services where symptoms are often considered along a continuum rather than in relation to thresholds that define disorder. Social impairment may occur in association with symptoms and will usually be present in association with psychiatric disorder (Hodes 2002a).

2. Do young refugees have specific symptoms and psychiatric disorders?

Refugee children may show behaviour and have disturbances and disorders that are provoked by specific experiences. Acute stress reactions, adjustment disorder, post-traumatic stress disorder and depression may be provoked by past adverse experiences. The presentation of these problems will vary according to the age of the children. Young children may be clingy, cry frequently and lose previously acquired skills such as bladder control. They may show preoccupation with violence or war images and in children this may be manifested in play or drawings. Children and adolescents may also experience repetitive and intrusive thoughts of the disturbing events, often with nightmares of these events, avoidance of reminders of these events and also high arousal. They may have poor concentration and disruptive behaviour.

It should be remembered that refugee children may also have disorders that could have occurred if they had never become refugees and migrated, such as neurodevelopmental abnormalities, e.g. autism, severe learning difficulties, and severe psychiatric disorders such as psychoses (Howard and Hodes 2000).

3. Are psychiatric disorders more common in refugee children?

Epidemiological studies of refugee children are beginning to be carried out in the UK. Emerging findings suggest higher risk of psychiatric disorder in refugee children compared with their peers (Fazel and Stein 2003). Many studies in other resettlement countries (mostly the USA, Canada and Sweden) suggest that the rates are higher than in non-refugee children (Hodes 2000). The rate of disorder is related to the degree of exposure to the various risk and protective factors, with greater risk associated with greater exposure. Thus children exposed to very directly threatening events and losses, such as those who have seen family members killed by soldiers, and perhaps experienced separation and detention or torture, will have very high risk of disorder. For example, among a group of adolescent survivors of the Khmer Rouge Pol Pot, most had post-traumatic disorder or affective disorders associated with significant social impairment (Kinzie, Sack, Angell, Manson and Ben 1986). Less extreme is a study of 50 young Iranian children, most of whom had been exposed to bombardment from missiles or seen assaults on parents (Almquist and Broberg 1999). The children left Iran, on average aged five years. When first seen 12 months after arrival in Sweden, 74 per cent were regarded as having poor psychological adjustment. A Canadian study of adolescents who had largely not been exposed to war violence found rates of psychiatric disorder, mainly conduct and depressive disorder, to be almost twice the rate of disorder (21 per cent) compared with non-refugee peers (11 per cent) (Tousignant, Habimana, Biron, Malo, Sidoli-LeBlanc and Bendris 1999).

4. Why do many refugee children exposed to adversities not appear highly distressed nor have symptoms or psychiatric disorders?

There many reasons why some refugee children are more resilient than others (Hodes 2000; Rutter 1987, 1999). There may be individual factors such as genetic predisposition or temperament that protect them. For others, cognitive style and coping may be more adaptive (Punamaki 1996). Children will also be protected by warm relationships with parents, and parents who have good coping and mental health. Community support and involvement may also be protective. There are also some specific factors that increase risk. Intrafamilial violence may contribute to the onset of childhood disturbance (Garbarino and Kostelny 1996), and loss caused by disappearance where there is uncertainty about death is more distressing for children and adults than certain knowledge of death, because of the impossibility of grieving (Quirk and Casco 1994).

Interventions

Some of the salient issues are described here, but fuller accounts are available (Ahearn and Athey 1991; in the UK context see Hodes 2002b). Interventions can be considered at three levels:

1. Community support

Given the dependency of young children on parents and families, supporting whole families and communities is important. The availability of legal aid, financial support or preferably employment, appropriate accommodation, access to health and schools for children will all have an influence on the welfare of families. Many asylum-seeking families find life in the UK a constant struggle in order to overcome hurdles in these aspects of living. When refugee status has been obtained, which is usually associated with greater time of settlement in the UK, then these obstacles usually reduce substantially. Nevertheless, working in child mental health these welfare problems are frequently raised and the practitioner will often be asked to have an advocacy role and prepare reports to support applications for asylum, housing or other needs. Over a period of years, many refugee families will establish their own informal networks which can be called on for advice, support and counselling. Despite the mobility of this population, sometimes more established organisations can develop which welcome and help newly arrived asylum seekers.

2. Universal interventions

Universal interventions are important for promoting the welfare of asylum-seeking and refugee children. These may involve education where teachers have important roles in settling in the children with induction programmes, language classes etc. (Richman 1998). Other professionals may help with school access. For younger children, health visitors may play an important role in visiting families in hotels or other homeless accommodation and helping with infancy problems including adjustment disorders. Organisations in the voluntary sector may also provide relevant support. In recent years the Government's social inclusion policies and substantial funding should be used to address the needs of refugee children (Hodes 2002b).

3. Child and adolescent mental health services

Given the numbers of asylum-seeking and refugee families in certain areas, and resource limitations, a tiered system in line with national child and adolescent mental health service plans is important (Health Advisory Service 1995). Tier 2 community-based mental health professionals in schools, social services or centres used by refugee families can provide consultation to Tier 1 professionals, carry a small caseload and refer appropriate children to Tier 3 services (O'Shea, Hodes, Down and Bramley 2000; Hodes 2002b). This may help overcome some of the barriers to accessing health care, including mobility and language and cultural barriers, that could occur by relying on general practitioner referral. Ideally, community-based child mental health professionals can be appointed specifically to work with young refugees.

A significant number of refugee children will be referred to specialist Tier 3 child mental health services. As indicated above, refugee children may have a range of problems that will require a multidisciplinary team. Our study in West London found that the referred refugee children may be as impaired as non-refugee ethnic minority and White British children, but tend to have more psychosocial problems (Howard and

Hodes 2000). The refugee children are more likely to be referred by schools and social workers than GPs or paediatricians and, despite more frequent need for interpreters, are no more likely to drop out of treatment.

A very small number of young refugees, but more than would be expected based on their numbers in the community, require psychiatric admission (Tier 4) (Tolmac and Hodes, submitted). These children and adolescents have complex psychiatric and psychosocial difficulties, including lower levels of family support.

Fuller accounts of treatment issues are available elsewhere (Hodes 2000; Westermeyer 1991). Young asylum seekers and refugees may have been exposed to organised violence, detention or torture, or interrogation which affects how they experience treatment. For example, clinical interviewing may remind them of past abuses. Some families and youngsters may be able to talk and obtain relief from communicating about these experiences, through speech, drawing or play. For others inquiring about past experiences may substantially increase arousal and trigger flashbacks. Sometimes it is necessary to avoid discussion of the past and focus on current difficulties. This may create tension for the therapist whose model for dealing with current distress may be to explore the past (Papadopoulos 1999). Over time, as the family becomes less distressed and trust is built up towards the therapist, it may then be possible to explore the past events. Frequently interpreters are needed and it is important for clinicians to be able to work effectively with them (Phelan and Parkman 1995).

As indicated above, young refugees may have any psychiatric disorder or problems, including learning difficulties. In view of this they will need access to a range of treatments. In community settings where adjustment problems and reactions to adverse social experiences are common, support to parents, obtaining appropriate resources, exploration of problems and improving parenting are frequently used interventions. For more severe and persistent interventions, drawing on evidence-based principles for interventions is desirable (Harrington, Kerfoot and Verduyn 1999). Nevertheless, these treatment options will need to be adapted to the cultural background and values of the families. Group interventions in community or clinic settings for selected children may be useful, and may 'normalise' many of the experiences and feelings of these youngsters. Cognitive therapy for post-traumatic stress disorder and depression is very useful. Such interventions may be provided to individuals, or in the presence of parents, who may also benefit from the interventions and support the child. Family therapy and an understanding of the effect of adverse experiences on families is important (Woodcock 2001). Some children benefit from drug treatments for more severe disorders such as psychoses. Occasionally drug treatments are required for treatment of post-traumatic stress disorder, usually when there is concurrent depression and high suicide risk (Davidson 2000).

Useful organisations

Medical Foundation for the Victims of Torture

Web site: http://www.torturecare.org.uk

Centre in North London that provides health services, including mental health services, and medical and legal reports for asylum seekers and refugees.

Refugee Council

Web site: http://www.refugeecouncil.org.uk

Provides information for asylum seekers and professionals about many aspects of their welfare.

United Nations High Commission for Refugees

Web site: http://www.unhcr.ch

Provides information about the worlds' refugees and displaced people.

Amnesty International

Web site: http://www.amnesty.org

Leading campaign organisation for the rights of political detainees and prisoners.

Refugee Studies Centre, University of Oxford

Web site: http://www.qeh.ox.ac.uk/rsp/

Leading academic centre in UK for the study of all aspects of refugees.

References

Ahearn, F. and Athey, J.L. (1991) *Refugee Children. Theory, Research and Services.* Baltimore and London: The Johns Hopkins University Press.

Aldous. J., Bardsley, M., Daniell, R., Gair, R., Jacobson, B., Lowdell, C., Morgan, D., Storkey, M. and Taylor, G. (1999) *Refugee Health in London. Key Issues for Public Health.* East London and The City Health Authority: The Health of Londoners Project.

Almquist, K. and Broberg, A.G. (1999) 'Mental health and social adjustment in young refugee children 3½ years after their arrival in Sweden.' *Journal of the American Academy of Child and Adolescent Psychiatry 38*, 723–730.

Davidson, J.R. (2000) 'Pharmacotherapy of post-traumatic stress disorder: treatment options, long-term follow-up, and predictors of outcome.' *Journal of Clinical Psychiatry 61*, 52–56.

Eisenbruch, M. (1991) 'From post-traumatic stress disorder to cultural bereavement: diagnosis of Southeast Asian refugees.' *Social Science and Medicine 33*, 673–680.

Fazel, M. and Stein, A. (2003) 'Mental health of refugee children: comparative study.' *British Medical Journal 327*, 134.

Garbarino, J. and Kostelny, K. (1996) 'The effects of political violence on Palestinian children's behavioural problems: a risk accumulation model.' *Child Development 67*, 33–45.

Gorst-Unsworth, C. and Goldenberg, E. (1998) 'Psychological sequelae of torture and organised violence suffered by refugees from Iraq.' *British Journal of Psychiatry 172*, 90–94.

Harrington, R.C., Kerfoot, M. and Verduyn, C. (1999) 'Developing needs-led child and adolescent mental health services: issues and prospects.' *European Journal of Child and Adolescent Psychiatry 8*, 1–10.

Health Advisory Service (1995) *Child and Adolescent Mental Health Services. Together We Stand.* London: HMSO.

Hodes, M. (2000) 'Psychologically distressed refugee children in the United Kingdom.' *Child Psychology and Psychiatry Review 5*, 57–68.

Hodes, M. (2002a) 'Three key issues for young refugees' mental health.' *Transcultural Psychiatry 39*, 196–213.

Hodes, M. (2002b) 'Implications for psychiatric services of chronic civilian strife or war: young refugees in the UK.' *Advances in Psychiatric Treatment 8*, 366–376.

Hodes, M. and Goldberg, D. (2002) 'The treatment of refugees: service provision reflects Britain's ambivalence.' *Psychiatric Bulletin 26*, 1–2.

Howard, M. and Hodes, M. (2000) 'Psychopathology, adversity, and service utilisation of young refugees.' *Journal of the American Academy of Child and Adolescent Psychiatry 39*, 368–377.

Kinzie, J.D., Sack, W.H., Angell, R.H., Manson, S. and Ben, R. (1986) 'The psychiatric effects of massive trauma on Cambodian children: I. The children.' *Journal of the American Academy of Child Psychiatry 25*, 370–376.

Kushner, T. and Knox, K. (1999) *The Age of Genocide.* London: Frank Cass.

Montgomery, E. (1998) 'Refugee Children from the Middle East.' *Scandinavian Journal of Social Medicine,* Supplementum 54.

O'Shea, B., Hodes, M., Down, G., and Bramley, J. (2000) 'A school based mental health service for refugee children.' *Clinical Child Psychology and Psychiatry 5*, 189–201.

Papadopoulos, R. (1999) 'Working with Bosnian medical evacuees and their families: therapeutic dilemmas.' *Clinical Child Psychiatry and Psychology 4*, 107–120.

Phelan, M. and Parkman, S. (1995) 'Work with an interpreter.' *British Medical Journal 311*, 555–557.

Punamaki, R.-L. (1996) 'Can ideological commitment protect children's psychosocial well-being in situations of political violence?' *Child Development 67*, 55–69.

Quirk G.J. and Casco, L. (1994) 'Stress disorders of families of the disappeared: a controlled study in Honduras.' *Social Science and Medicine 39*, 1675–1679.

Refugee Council (2001) *Where are the children?* London: Refugee Council and British Agencies for Adoption and Fostering.

Refugee Council (2002) *Refugee council briefing.* London: Refugee Council.

Richman, N. (1998) *In the midst of the whirlwind.* Stoke-on-Trent: Trentham Books.

Rousseau, C. (1995) 'The mental health of refugee children.' *Transcultural Psychiatric Research Review 32*, 299–331.

Rutter, M. (1987) 'Psychosocial resilience and protective mechanisms.' *American Journal of Orthopsychiatry 57*, 316–331.

Rutter, M. (1999) 'Resilience concepts and findings: implications for family therapy.' *Journal of Family Therapy 21*, 119–144.

Sack, W. (1998) 'Multiple forms of stress in refugee and immigrant children.' *Child and Adolescent Psychiatric Clinics of North America 7*, 153–167.

Summerfield, D. (2000a) 'Childhood, war, refugeedom and "trauma": Three core questions for mental health professionals.' *Transcultural Psychiatry 37*, 417–433.

Summerfield, D. (2000b) 'War and mental health: a brief overview.' *British Medical Journal 321*, 232–235.

Tolmac, J. and Hodes, M. (submitted) *Ethnicity and adolescent psychiatric admission for psychotic disorders.*

Tousignant, M., Habimana, E., Biron, C., *Malo, C.*, Sidoli-LeBlanc, C. and Bendris, N. (1999) 'The Quebec adolescent refugee project: Psychopathology and family variables in a sample from 35 nations.' *Journal of the American Academy of Child and Adolescent Psychiatry 38*, 1426–1432.

UNHCR (2000) *The State of the World's Refugees. Fifty Years of Humanitarian Action.* Oxford: Oxford University Press.

Westermeyer, J. (1991) 'Psychiatric services for refugee children.' In F. Ahearn and J.L. Athey (eds) *Refugee children. Theory, research and services* pp.127–162. Baltimore and London: The Johns Hopkins University Press.

Woodcock, J. (2001) 'Threads from the labyrinth: therapy with survivors of war and political oppression.' *Journal of Family Therapy 23*, 136–154.

World Health Organisation (1992) *The ICD-10 Classification of Mental and Behavioural Disorders.* Geneva: World Health Organisation.

World Health Organisation (1996) *Multiaxial classification of child and adolescent psychiatric disorders. The ICD-10 classification of mental and behavioural disorders in children and adolescents.* Cambridge: Cambridge University Press.

Part Two

Survey Methods and Findings

Under the NHS reforms, Primary Care Trusts/Groups (PCTs) will take responsibility for commissioning needs assessments in their role as commissioners of services. These changes were under way at the time of the FOCUS survey and Primary Care Trusts/Groups were established in some participating areas.

Until now, there has been little opportunity to review practice relating to CAMHS provision for minority ethnic groups. Without any baseline information, it is difficult for services to 'benchmark' their practice against that of other organisations. The literature presented in Part 1 of this report highlights the importance of commissioning bodies and service providers in the planning and delivery of appropriate services. With that in mind FOCUS selected and interviewed commissioners and Tier 3 CAMHS managers in order to gauge current practice. We aimed to gain further insights into current planning and provision of CAMHS for minority ethnic groups as well as to highlight areas of good or innovative practice.

We would like to thank all the people involved in this survey for their time and honesty in responding to the questionnaires.

Survey methods

Separate interview schedules were devised for CAMHS commissioners and Tier 3 respondents (see Appendix IV) and were administered by telephone interviews. A semi-structured interview method was used, and interview schedules included a combination of 'open' and 'closed' questions.

Selection of survey sample

Initial considerations about CAMHS provision highlighted that the structure and provision of CAMHS across England, Scotland, Wales and Ireland varied. It was therefore necessary to concentrate on CAMHS provision in England and to ensure that respondents were selected from areas with high, mid and low concentration of minority ethnic groups in the local population.

Data from the 1991 Census regarding the ethnic make-up of local authorities was used to create a database. Local authorities were ordered according to the total number of minority ethnic groups in the population, from those with the highest number to the lowest. Five of the 15 local authorities in England were then randomly selected from this sampling frame, ensuring that a cross section of those with high, mid and low numbers of minority ethnic groups were included.

A similar procedure was adopted for London which has the highest concentration of minority ethnic groups in England; 32 inner and outer London boroughs are listed in the 1991 Census. Of these, 12 boroughs were selected, six each from inner and outer London, again ensuring that those selected were representative of differing numbers of minority ethnic groups in both inner and outer London boroughs.

Identifying respondents

There is no central source from which CAMHS commissioners and Tier 3 team managers or equivalent can be identified. To access this information, the Department of Health recommended contacting Regional Health Leads in the selected areas. It was possible to identify CAMHS commissioners through this route, and some Tier 3 managers. The majority of Tier 3 managers, however, were identified through CAMHS commissioners.

Final survey sample

The intention of the survey was to include all CAMHS commissioners and Tier 3 managers in the selected areas. One of the five local authorities was unable to participate within the timescale for this project and therefore the final number of local authorities participating was reduced to four. Details of local authorities, commissioners and Tier 3 team managers identified and the number participating are as follows:

Table II.1 Participating commissioners and service managers	
Local authorities and respondents	**Number**
Local authorities selected	5
Local authorities participating	4
CAMHS commissioners identified*	16
CAMHS commissioners participating	13
Tier 3 team managers identified*	20
Tier 3 team managers participating+	14

Key:

*The number of commissioners and Tier 3 team managers identified across all five local authorities selected.

+One manager was responsible for four teams in the survey areas at the time of interview. The number of CAMHS teams represented covered in the interviews is therefore 17.

Survey administration period

Telephone interviews with respondents were conducted between September and December 2001.

Analysis

It was recognised from the onset that a small-scale survey such as this could not claim to be representative or to acquire data that was conducive to statistical analysis. In order to gauge response categories, a coding system was devised and applied to quantitative and qualitative data collected. The codes were fed into a database to enable simple frequency counts to be obtained.

Limitations of survey

The summaries of findings presented in this section will provide readers with a 'snapshot' of current commissioning practice and service provision.

As stated above, a survey of this size cannot claim to be truly representative of practice throughout England or indeed the United Kingdom.

The findings presented that relate to service provision are the views of the managers from a range of services and may not represent the views of other professionals within those teams.

Survey findings

What sources do commissioners use to obtain profiles of local minority ethnic groups?

The national source of data cited was the Census; all other sources are local. The most frequently used sources were health authority or Trust statistics (seven respondents) and the Census (five respondents). All those who cited the Census also supplemented this data with local sources, but not all those using local sources supplemented this with Census or other national data. It is possible that local sources were considered to be more appropriate and/or sufficient.

A very different approach was highlighted by one respondent; that of looking at whole communities and considering the profile of minority ethnic groups within this. This was said to be a better approach than using national sources such as the Census which would not identify some local minority groups, in particular those of European origin.

Reasons for not using any sources

Two respondents who said that no sources were being used explained that they were aware of the gap that existed in relation to addressing the needs of minority ethnic groups. In both cases the respondents said they were looking to prioritise and address this following recent reorganisation of their services.

Table II.2 How data was used in commissioning	
To assess under or over representation	2
Data not used systematically	7
Not known (recent appointment)	1
Other	1

How do commissioners use this data in planning provision for local minority ethnic groups?

Of the 11 respondents who cited sources they used to obtain profiles of local minority ethnic groups, most said they did not use this data systematically.

How data was used

Three respondents were able to provide an indication about how the information was used; two of these said it was used to look at unmet needs:

> Highlights unmet needs so we can look at addressing these. For example, under- or over-representation in services.

One respondent added that some services were further ahead in addressing the issue of unmet needs than others.

Feedback from the third respondent (in the 'Other' category of Table II.2) illustrated a very different approach:

> Feedback from community groups goes to a forum that discusses issues emerging from the data. The forum then feeds data into development of services. The data is also used to access funding for establishing work that will address highlighted needs for particular minority ethnic groups.

Data not used systematically

Those stating that the data was not used systematically were either able to provide some insight as to why this might be the case or were unable to provide any explanation as to why this was the case.

AN AREA TO BE ADDRESSED IN THE FUTURE

This was the most frequent reason (five respondents) with one respondent highlighting that data needed to be more robust for it to be useful:

> The data is not used systematically and it is acknowledged that available data is not sufficiently robust to enable looking at needs. We are currently looking at ways of developing this area.

NO CLEAR EXPLANATION GIVEN

The remaining two respondents were unable to provide any clear indication as to why data was not used, for example:

> X is a very heterogeneous area and there is a recognition that different groups require specialist input, but a lot more actually needs to be done in addressing needs.

Do commissioners consider the data they collect to be adequate for planning services for minority ethnic groups?

Asked to indicate on a five-point scale (from 'very adequate' to 'very inadequate') the extent to which respondents found the sources of information they used to be adequate, only two selected 'adequate'. Six out of 13 of the respondents selected 'don't know' either because they did not use any sources or because they did not use them systematically, or were new in post. Four out of 13 found the sources they used to be less than adequate.

Data considered adequate and suggestions for improvement

None of the respondents considered the sources they used to be 'very adequate'. Two found them to be adequate and one other respondent selected adequate for some sources and inadequate for others. Comments and suggestions about the limitations of available data and how data could be improved are as follows.

DATA NEEDS TO BE ROBUST AND RELEVANT TO HEALTH PROVISION

The need for accurate and relevant information is illustrated by the following comments:

> Borough data (such as statistics of the local school population) is more robust than Health Trust data, but is limited because it is not designed for health purposes. Census and Trust Activity statistics

provide an overall picture but need supplementing because they are not useful for all aspects of planning.

Some of the Census data and consultations with the local community is useful for planning and/or securing funding. However, available data is not always sufficient or relevant.

DATA FOR INTER-AGENCY PLANNING

Though the use of data for inter-agency planning was not a focus of this survey, one respondent did highlight difficulties encountered in this area:

Another issue concerns discrepancies in data collection between agencies, which does not facilitate inter-agency planning. Some of the difficulties could be addressed through developing IT systems that enable better collation and analysis.

CLIENT FEEDBACK

One respondent used client feedback, obtained by the CAMHS service in the area, as a source of information for service planning and cited this source as the most useful.

Feedback from clients (who they are and what they want) is the most useful data.

Ways in which data sources considered inadequate

Respondents who found the data to be inadequate or very inadequate gave the following reasons as to why they thought this was the case.

LACK OF RELIABILITY

Unreliability of data sources was said to relate to inaccuracy of information about ethnicity and insufficient robustness.

Health Trust statistics are incomplete (if services don't return data) and unreliable in relation to ethnicity (some staff 'guess' the ethnicity of the client).

Census and health authority statistics are not robust enough, are inaccurate and do not take account of diversity or provide information relating to the needs of particular groups.

OTHER LIMITATIONS OF SOURCES USED

The following points were made in relation to why Census and health authority data was considered inadequate for planning services or interventions:

- The sources only provided information relating to the main ethnic categories; no data was available about subgroups falling outside of these categories.

- No data was available in these sources about mental health conditions or epidemiology.

- The statistics did not enable cross-tabulation of variables, for example, the number of four-year-olds from the Bangladeshi community.

- Census, local demographic and school population data was said to be difficult to interpret for CAMHS planning purposes.

It is apparent from these responses that greater consideration needs to be given to the development of information systems and approaches that provide relevant and reliable data.

Do commissioners undertake an assessment of needs for the local minority ethnic group population?

Needs assessments are described as a vital aspect of the commissioning process to address the needs of local populations; considering particular needs such as those of minority ethnic groups are an important aspect of this process (Rawaf 1998). It is also suggested that to be useful, needs assessments should be updated regularly to take account of changes in the structure of the local populations and their needs (Bahl 1998).

Types of needs assessments undertaken

Only three out of 12 respondents said they undertook these assessments, giving the following responses:

Ethnicity is taken into account as part of wider CAMHS needs assessments.

An (one-off) assessment was commissioned ... but not completed due to the post becoming vacant. It will resume pending new appointment.

We are currently looking to develop this in the newly established Primary Care Trust.

Interestingly this feedback is similar to that given by respondents saying no assessments were undertaken, as outlined below under 'Needs assessments not undertaken'. This may suggest a difference in criteria used to assess whether assessments of need are undertaken for local minority ethnic groups. It is also possible that some general assessments are perceived, rightly or wrongly, as being sufficient approaches to assessing the needs of particular groups.

Needs assessments not undertaken

Of the nine respondents who said that needs assessments were not undertaken for local minority ethnic groups:

- Four respondents said that assessments of the local population were undertaken and local minority ethnic groups would be included; however, assessments did not adopt a specific approach to highlighting the needs of minority ethnic groups. Respondents were unclear as to why this was the case.

- Three respondents said they were aware of the need for such assessments and would be looking to develop this area in future.

- One respondent indicated that a one-off analysis had been undertaken in the last year and the multi-agency group that commissioned it would consider the data gathered.

- Another respondent highlighted the need to get baseline data sufficiently robust first and this would then enable more thorough needs assessments.

When the last assessment was undertaken

Of the three respondents who said needs assessments were undertaken in their localities, each highlighted different time periods for when the last assessment had been commissioned or undertaken:

- In one locality this had been commissioned 18 months previously but was still to be completed.

- In another the last assessment was undertaken three years previously.

• The third locality had undertaken an assessment two years previously.

Whether the assessments were focused on general populations, or minority ethnic groups in particular, these timescales vary considerably. Further exploration is needed about the extent to which targeted assessments are needed and the regularity with which they need to be undertaken.

How do commissioners use the data from needs assessments?

Only one respondent was able to provide a concrete example of how data from assessments undertaken was used. Though the assessment was not targeted at minority ethnic groups, it highlighted a gap in provision for this group. As a result of this finding, a counsellor was appointed to develop work with young people from minority ethnic groups. Subsequent to this appointment, the number of young people from minority ethnic groups attending for counselling was said to have doubled.

Do commissioners have up-to-date information about the local minority ethnic group population?

Securing services that meet the needs of minority ethnic groups should be a core aspect of the commissioning process (Chandra 1996).

It is suggested that accurate and reliable data to assess needs may be obtained from a variety of sources. These may include primary (e.g. surveys) and secondary (e.g. data already collected, such as service utilisation data) sources, evaluations of interventions and knowledge held by other agencies and professionals including those in the voluntary sector.

The FOCUS survey aimed to establish whether commissioners had up-to-date information, obtained through needs assessments or otherwise, on some key areas of local minority ethnic groups' awareness and take-up of services. The areas in question and commissioner responses are summarised in Table II.3.

Do you have up-to-date information about local minority ethnic groups in relation to…?

Few commissioners had up-to-date information about the areas highlighted in Table II.3. The qualitative responses of those who said they had this infor-

Table II.3 Up-to-date information			
Area of information relating to local minority ethnic groups	Yes	No	Other
Minority ethnic groups' awareness of mental health issues	1	11	1
Minority ethnic groups' awareness of mental health services	1	11	1
Minority ethnic groups' access to services	3	8	2
Types of services taken up	1	9	3
Discrepancies in types of services taken up	1	9	3

mation indicate that, in fact, some respondents were unclear as to whether this data was available and others questioned the reliability of available information.

Sources of available information

The Contract Minimum Data Set (CMDS) database was cited by some respondents as the source of up-to-date information. The CMDS introduced classification by ethnic group in 1995 and is described as an essential tool in the development of effective commissioning (Bahl 1998).

Respondents who cited this source had reservations about its reliability in relation to data on minority ethnic groups and did not necessarily use it. For example:

> The CMDS database can be manipulated to obtain information about these (access, type of services taken up, discrepancies in types of service taken up) but its reliability is questionable and available data is not always sufficient.

> It is possible to access CMDS data collected by the health authority that would enable this to be worked out but its reliability is questionable.

Other sources related to data about minority ethnic groups' awareness of mental health and mental health services. Two respondents thought data relating to these aspects was possibly being collected through specialist initiatives aimed at the overall client group, for example:

> This information is likely being collected under a current initiative that aims to raise awareness and access. It is targeted at communities and where minority ethnic groups are a part of that community their needs would be taken into account.

The above qualitative feedback illustrates that where data is available, its reliability is questioned and its availability does not necessarily mean that it is used. This issue was highlighted by the Office for Public Management (1996), that where information was available it did not necessarily lead to action.

Data not available/used

The majority of respondents said they did not have up-to-date information about the areas in question. Some of their feedback, in relation to information sources, indicates similar concerns to those given by respondents who said they did have this information. For example:

> Various sources can provide this information but there is no targeted approach or regular updating.

> Any available information is anecdotal.

> Any information available on any of these issues is likely to be patchy and not necessarily focused on minority ethnic groups.

Other feedback highlights issues relating to lack of information sharing and the need to develop this area in future, for minority ethnic groups as well as the overall client group. For example:

> The Trust may have information relevant to these areas but it is not passed on to commissioners.

> Hope to develop this area in the future now the PCTs are established and operational.

> This is not done for CAMHS generally.

Do commissioners undertake regular reviews of service provision for minority ethnic groups?

Setting quality standards for the health of minority ethnic groups, monitoring progress and taking forward findings highlighted by regular reviews are an essential component of ensuring quality services, including the commissioning process (Bahl 1998; Rawaf 1998). The FOCUS survey was therefore interested to establish with commissioners whether regular reviews were undertaken in relation to the following key aspects of CAMHS provision for minority ethnic groups:

- mental health promotion
- identification of mental health problems
- assessment of mental health problems
- the appropriateness of services to meet current needs
- the effectiveness of the interventions provided.

No regular reviews were indicated in relation to CAMHS provision to minority ethnic groups. There was an indication from some respondents that general reviews may take into account service provision to minority ethnic groups. For example:

> Just beginning to look at the area of reviews. Reviews are undertaken on various issues as and when time permits. Some reviews are not targeted at minority ethnic groups, but their situation would be highlighted through looking at the general population.

> The last review of CAMHS was undertaken by the local health authority two or three years ago and another is due to start later this year. Needs of minority ethnic groups would be looked at as part of this.

> There are regular reviews but these are not focused on minority ethnic groups. So, some of this information will be available but it is not clear to what extent this is reliable or exactly which areas it covers.

Two respondents said they were looking to address this issue in the future and another highlighted difficulties in relation to undertaking regular reviews:

> This area has a hugely transient population so the local demography can change quite rapidly and there are insufficient resources to enable regular reviews.

It is unclear from this data the extent to which general reviews are sufficient in assessing provision to minority ethnic groups in particular. However, the need to consider how the undertaking of regular reviews can be supported and data used to inform future developments in provision for minority ethnic groups is apparent.

Do commissioners provide any guidelines to providers about addressing the mental health needs of clients from minority ethnic groups?

This question does not relate to specifications/contracts, which are addressed later.

It is suggested that commissioners can support providers to understand and address the needs of local communities (Bahl 1998). One of the ways in which this can be achieved is by way of commissioners communicating the needs of local communities to providers in order to facilitate them in developing appropriate services.

Ten out of 11 respondents did not provide any guidelines to providers. Indeed, the one respondent who gave an affirmative answer went on to say that nothing specific was provided in relation to particular groups.

> There is a general clause that requires providers to ensure equal access, but nothing specific for particular groups.

This response is similar to those of others who said no guidelines were provided. Feedback from respondents indicating that no guidelines were provided, highlights a range of reasons as to why this was the case, for example:

Not the responsibility of commissioners

> This is not the responsibility of commissioners. Providers should have their own guidelines and know that they need to address the needs of their client group.

Provision of guidelines not considered

> Only state that sensitivity should be applied and interpreters used where necessary. This is not something we have thought about.

> Don't know why this is the case.

Recognition of need to develop guidelines in future

> Will be looking to develop this area over the coming year.

> This is an area that needs to be addressed for CAMHS generally and minority ethnic groups in particular.

Provision of guidelines not recognised as relevant

> Local authority view is likely to be that this is because of the low number of minority ethnic groups in the local population (less than 1 per cent). This is not a personal view and it should not be the case.

These responses highlight that the issuing of guidelines to assist providers in addressing the needs of minority ethnic groups have either received insufficient attention or are considered not to be relevant. Such differences in opinion indicate the need for this issue to be debated further so that the issuing of guidelines, or not, is based on informed and appropriate criteria.

Do commissioners specify requirements, in service specifications or contracts with providers, about the provision of services to address the mental health needs of local minority ethnic groups?

The commissioning process can be used to specify the delivery of culturally competent services. Requirements in this respect can be stipulated in service specifications/contracts with providers (Bahl 1998).

Of the 11 respondents who specified requirements, seven said they did not specify requirements to providers in relation to addressing the needs of minority ethnic groups. Feedback from those who did specify requirements highlights a number of approaches.

Requirements specified

The four commissioners who said they did specify requirements highlighted that these were in addition to a general clause requiring providers to ensure equal access for all groups. The nature of specific requirements specified for minority ethnic groups are as follows.

REQUIREMENTS SPECIFIED WHEN CONSIDERED NECESSARY

One commissioner highlighted that specific requirements were agreed with providers who were commissioned to address identified needs:

> In addition to the general clause, specific services will be commissioned to address particular needs where these are identified. Where appropriate, more generic services will be asked to address the needs of particular groups. Requirements in addition to the general clause are agreed as appropriate.

REQUIREMENTS SPECIFIED IN RELATION TO OVER-REPRESENTED GROUPS

The lack of awareness about the needs of minority ethnic groups was highlighted as an obstacle, by another commissioner, in specifying requirements other than for minority ethnic groups who were over-represented.

> In addition to the general clause, specifications will be made of providers in relation to needs of groups that are over-represented, e.g. mental health of young people from minority ethnic groups who are looked after. The general clause does not cover needs of all minority ethnic groups because we are not aware of all their needs.

RELIANCE ON NEEDS ASSESSMENTS

Feedback from a third commissioner highlighted specifications at Tier 4; other than this there was a reliance on needs assessments to ensure appropriate provision.

> Services must be based on assessment of local need. Minority ethnic groups are not specified so this is implicit rather than explicit. User involvement is promoted. Contracts with Tier 4 providers specify requirements to meet religious and dietary needs.

MINORITY ETHNIC GROUPS NAMED IN QUALITY STANDARDS REQUIREMENTS

The fourth respondent who said requirements were specified highlighted that this was done under quality standards requirements. Providers were also asked for data on service use and ethnicity was one of the areas in which information was requested.

> Quality standards are required under which minority ethnic groups are one named group whose needs must be addressed. Providers are requested to submit analysis of service use/provision by age, gender and ethnicity of staff team as well as clients.

No requirements specified

Seven respondents said that other than a general clause requiring providers to ensure equal access to all groups, no further requirements were specified. Three of these respondents added that this was an area they hoped to develop in future.

Do commissioners use providers from the voluntary/community sector?

A recent study commissioned by the Department of Health (Singh 1998), recommended that health agencies should work with relevant voluntary sector agencies to address the needs of minority ethnic groups. A range of opportunities for voluntary sector involvement were highlighted including their contribution to the development of commissioning strategies. Service provision by voluntary agencies is also encouraged both in relation to general health and CAMHS in particular (Bhui, Christie and Bhugra 1995; Chandra 1996; House of Commons Health Committee 1997; Kurtz, Thornes and Wolkind 1994; Malek 1997).

All 13 respondents said they did use providers from this sector. The reasons for this were said to be because services in this sector had a particular expertise and clients from minority ethnic groups appeared more likely to engage with them. Some commissioners demonstrated a more structured approach to using providers from the voluntary sector than others.

> This borough has a policy to have a mixed economy of provision. Voluntary services are able to engage clients in a way that Child and Family Consultation Clinics are not. Minority ethnic groups don't access statutory services as readily as those in the voluntary sector.

> Clients find these services more accessible (than statutory CAMHS).

Use a lot of voluntary services – clients appear to be more likely to return to voluntary services and sustained input/engagement of clients appears to be more effective in this sector.

Overall the statutory services do not have the capacity to address specialist needs, whereas voluntary/community groups have developed particular expertise in meeting specialist needs.

Currently, this is not done systematically and there is a need to be more organised in working with the voluntary sector. The links at present are patchy and operate on an as-needed basis.

What do commissioners think would improve the provision of services for local minority ethnic groups?

All respondents made suggestions that relate to the need for better informa-tion, resources, awareness, needs assessments, client feedback, inter-agency work and service developments.

Information

Suggestions relating to information needs were:

- data that is more accurate, reliable, takes account of diverse communities and is relevant to CAMHS

- a central source from which data can be accessed

- greater support from the Department of Health in collecting and accessing the data

- better use of information already collected.

Resources

Extra resources were said to be needed in order to:

- Address the needs of diverse communities. It was said to be particularly difficult in areas that had a high degree of diversity to address the needs of all minority groups to a satisfactory level within limited resources.

- Develop specialist work and approaches to address the needs of minority ethnic groups. Some CAMHS were said to be underfunded overall and this could result in the needs of particular groups not being addressed. For example, one service was aware of the need to develop outreach work with certain local minority ethnic groups who were under-represented in the service. However, this work was unlikely to take place until necessary resources were available.

- Facilitate the development of mainstream CAMHS to provide a better service to all clients including those from minority ethnic groups.

Awareness

Some commissioners highlighted the need for better knowledge and understanding about:

- potential client population from minority ethnic groups
- potential needs in the client population that are specific to minority ethnic groups
- gaps in service provision for minority ethnic groups.

Needs assessments

Several suggestions were made in relation to undertaking or improving needs assessments:

- Enter into a dialogue with minority ethnic groups to identify needs.
- Evaluate current provision against identified needs.
- Undertake more thorough assessments of need than had been undertaken previously.
- Act on the outcome of needs assessment once completed.
- Acquire a better understanding of needs; current understanding is quite superficial.

Inter-agency work

Some developments were suggested in relation to facilitating better inter-agency work:

- There should be more sharing, discussion and debate of developments and good practice with other services.

- There should be greater acknowledgement (than there is at present) from statutory agencies to work with voluntary services.

- Frontline staff should have better information about where to refer clients for specialist support. Some frontline staff were said to have limited information about appropriate interventions they could seek out for clients from minority ethnic groups.

Consolidating developments

After the recent rounds of restructuring in the NHS it was felt that the developments should be consolidated and future ones prioritised, on a county-wide level (looking at tiers of provision) as well as more locally (looking at needs of whole communities).

Address issues raised by the survey

One respondent said it was important to look at areas that had been raised by the questions asked during this survey interview.

All commissioners expressed a desire to improve provision for minority ethnic groups and a willingness to address issues that would facilitate this. There was also some acknowledgement that certain issues needed to be prioritised and addressed within local strategies and structures but others required greater support from relevant central government departments.

Table 11.4 How minority ethnic groups were defined by service managers	
By Census or health body categories	2
By client self-definition only	1
By both categories and client self-definition	5
Health body definition not known; personal definition given	2
Other	4

How is ethnicity defined?

Given that ethnicity may be defined in a number of ways, it was important to ascertain from respondents how this was addressed in their services. The responses were varied for both sets of respondents. However, there was a marked difference between service managers and CAMHS commissioners in their awareness of how ethnicity was defined in the workplace.

Commissioners

Eleven of the 13 commissioners interviewed said they did not know how their health body (authority or Trust) defined minority ethnic groups. Uncertainty also exists in distinguishing between ethnic category and ethnic identity.

Service managers

The significant part played by categories based on datasets such as the Census is apparent. Only one respondent provided a definition that was not linked to the manner in which ethnicity was recorded:

> Clients from different countries who are resident in Britain and who have specific cultural, religious and linguistic characteristics that are different from the majority White population and that may require specialist intervention.

The qualitative data illustrates some uncertainty as well as some examples of how the issue of ethnic category and ethnic identity are addressed. For example:

Responses illustrating uncertainty

> I guess by determining those groups of people who are not indigenous.

> Those who are not British-born White. This is a confusing area because some would include only Black people in this group. Ethnicity should not relate to skin colour only.

> Can't say – the referral form has categories which referrers complete before making a referral. This service does not have any input into that.

Responses indicating more clarity

> According to categories provided by the Trust and based on Census categories.

> Clients self-identify and this is recorded on client file. The self-identity data is then standardised for feeding into the computer. Computer data and file data are therefore different.

> Categories based on DoH guidance sheet are used for planning purposes. Local minority groups not included in the guidance are added on (e.g. White European communities).

> Clients are asked to self-identify and sometimes referrers will provide this information. If there is a discrepancy, the client definition is recorded.

There was also some indication that different CAMHS teams within a particular Trust or authority can differ in how they define minority ethnic groups. One respondent who at the time of interview was managing four Tier 3 teams gave the following feedback:

> Probably different teams have different definitions. Overall clients are asked to self-identify and this is fitted into categories for the Trust.

The significant part played by categories based on datasets such as the Census is apparent in the definitions and views given by both sets of respondents. It is also evident in the responses that some services are further ahead than others in addressing the need for information that can be standardised for administrative purposes and richer, more qualitative data needed for clinical intervention.

How is ethnicity data recorded?

Service managers

When asked if the ethnicity of clients was recorded, 12 service managers responded that it was recorded and two said that it was not recorded.

Reasons given for not collecting the data highlight either a lack of priority or inadequate information systems:

The services are supposed to, but the forms that ask for this information are tucked away at the back of the file and no one fills them in.

We are currently developing information systems so that ethnicity data can be collected in the future.

Which sources are used by services to record information relating to clients ethnicity?

Nine of the 12 CAMHS that recorded data relating to ethnicity asked the young person and/or parent carer for this information.

- The young person's age was cited as an important determinant of whether they or their parent/carer were the source of information about ethnicity. Adolescents were more likely to be seen on their own than younger children and young people seen on their own were asked to define themselves. Parents/carers were asked if they accompanied the young person or the young person was too young to define themselves.

- Though the young person or the parent/carer should have been the main source, this was not always the case in some services. In cases where referrers included details about client ethnicity, this was not always checked with clients (young person or parent/carer). Whether these details were checked with clients before recording on CAMHS files was up to individual clinicians and did not always happen.

- In one service parents were said to provide this information by selecting an ethnic category on the form they were required to complete on their first attendance at the clinic. This illustrates the need for consideration about what is actually meant by 'source'. In this service, the parent is the source because they select a category; they are, however, limited to categories that have been created and provided by another 'source'.

There is a likelihood of there being discrepancies between how individuals describe their own ethnicity as compared to descriptions given by other people. Indeed, three respondents pointed out that, in some cases, the young person's response to their ethnicity was different to that given by their parent/carer.

A number of sources of data is apparent as is the need for services to consider which source is the most appropriate. Referrer feedback about client ethnicity may not always be a reliable source.

What type of information is collected about client ethnicity by services?

Data relating to country of origin was collected by 12 of the 17 CAMHS that recorded client ethnicity. Additional data was also collected by ten of these services but there was no consistent pattern in the nature of other information collected.

'Country of origin data only'

The following feedback from one respondent illustrates the need to be aware of limitations that might apply in relation to client self-definition:

> The self-definition relates in some way to 'Country of origin', for example, Black British, Dual Heritage.

'Self-definition' may therefore be limited to particular aspects of ethnicity, especially if clients are asked to self-define by selecting from pre-defined categories.

Feedback from the other respondent in this category illustrates the need to be clear not only about the type of information needed, but also at which stage in the process of accessing services this is needed. For example:

> Categories on the referral form relate to the country of origin. Information about language spoken is not asked on the form, but referrers sometimes specify this on referral if an interpreter is likely to be required.

'Country of origin and other data'

Feedback provided by most respondents under this category (six) highlights two main purposes for collecting data on client ethnicity: administrative and clinical. Some services have developed approaches that appear to address both of these requirements while avoiding the need to ask clients to repeat details several times. Feedback from six respondents indicates that this is achieved by:

- Recording 'Country'-related data for administrative purposes, based on the self-description provided by the client, rather than staff asking an outright question or asking clients to select from a set of predetermined categories.

- For the purposes of clinical interventions a range of data such as religion, language spoken and cultural beliefs may be taken into account as relevant, but not necessarily collected routinely.

Clearly there is some element of bias in this approach because by deciding what data is to be collected/recorded, ultimately it is professionals, not clients, who also decide what is relevant. Nevertheless, this approach illustrates attempts being made to meet differing needs for information about client ethnicity, while aiming to exercise some sensitivity towards clients.

Data for inter-agency work

One respondent highlighted difficulties arising in relation to inter-agency planning when different agencies collected different types of data or collected it under different categories.

The 'Don't Know' category

In one service with a high concentration of minority ethnic groups in its catchment area, the 'Don't Know' category was highlighted as being significant. Here, 25 per cent of cases were said to be recorded under the category 'Don't Know' for the following reasons:

1. If client response did not fit a predetermined category it was recorded as 'Don't Know', for example, if client identified themselves by religion and not by one of the predetermined categories relating to country of origin.

2. If client refused to answer the question.

3. Clients otherwise slipped through the net, for example, if referrer or clinician did not bother to fill out this part of the form.

Services need to give careful consideration to the type of information that is collected about children and young people from minority ethnic groups.

How is client ethnicity data used by services to plan for service provision?

Half of the service managers said they did use the data collected to plan the provision of services. The remaining seven either did not use it, did not collect it or did not use it on any regular or systematic basis.

Reason for not using the data

One service manager highlighted that qualitative data obtained from client self-definition was said to be difficult to standardise and therefore was not used. This service was, however, giving consideration to how data collected from clients could be developed to make it useful for service planning.

Reasons for not using the data on a regular or systematic basis

The four services provided different insights about why data was not used regularly or systematically.

One service was in the process of reviewing how the data collected could be better used to inform future developments. One area to be considered was the appropriateness of information currently being collected and whether this needed to be reviewed to make it more useful for planning purposes.

In another service the data was not used systematically (on a regular or consistent basis) and this was considered to be unsatisfactory. It was unclear if this situation would be reviewed in future.

The feedback from another respondent highlighted issues relating to the differing needs of data for clinical work and for planning overall service provision. Here the data was used by clinicians to inform their work with individual clients but was not used for overall service provision. Another issue highlighted by this respondent was the lack of information about how data returned by the service to the trust was used by them.

Using the data to commission one-off pieces of work was highlighted by one respondent who also said the data was not used regularly. The last time the data was used was two years previously when low uptake of the service by minority ethnic groups was identified and a study was commissioned to look at the reasons for non-access. The study had in turn helped to secure short-term funding to undertake outreach work. However, this initiative was said to have ended when the funding period came to an end.

Ways in which data was used to plan the provision of services

A number of valuable insights were provided by respondents who said the data was used to plan provision of services. Some services cited more than one way in which the data was used.

TO ASSESS UNDER- OR OVER-REPRESENTATION IN SERVICE USE

This was the most frequently cited use of the data (five respondents). Assessing under- or over-representation was achieved by cross-referencing data collected by CAMHS services with other national (e.g. Census) and local (e.g. school population) statistics. This was said to inform thinking about future development of the service.

TO ORGANISE SPECIALIST SERVICES

Five respondents said having relevant data about the needs of minority ethnic groups was useful in accessing specialist support, for example, translation and interpreting or other specialist resources for particular groups of clients such as those who were asylum seekers.

TO INFORM STAFF RECRUITMENT

The data was used by two services to assess the extent to which ethnicity of staff reflected the local population and the client group of the service. This was then used to inform strategies for staff recruitment.

TO PLAN INTERVENTIONS WITH CLIENTS

Knowledge about the client's ethnicity was said by two respondents to be helpful to clinicians for planning appropriate intervention with their clients.

TO PLAN THE SERVICE SO IT MIRRORED THE CLIENT GROUP

Knowledge about clients was said to assist one team with their ongoing aim of developing a service that mirrored the client group needs in what it provides. This was said to apply to various aspects of service provision, from the decor of the building to planning appropriate interventions and outreach work.

TO INFORM RESEARCH

One respondent highlighted that research undertaken by the service was informed in part by the knowledge it gained about its clients. In addition to informing the work of the service, it was likely that published research would also assist CAMHS provision more generally.

The Trust in which one service was based had a specialist group set up to look at issues relating to ethnicity. Data collected by the service was fed into this group who took on the responsibility of addressing issues being raised by the data, for example staff recruitment and training.

Is the data collected adequate for planning the provision of services?

Respondents were asked about the extent to which they thought the data collected was adequate in planning the provision of services. They were asked to specify this on a five-point scale ranging from 'very adequate' to 'very inadequate'. Of the 12 CAMHS that collected data, eight service managers responded that the data collected was adequate for planning and provision of services, three thought the data was inadequate and one responded that data was collected but not used.

Ways in which ethnicity data considered adequate for service planning

Five of the eight respondents who thought the data was adequate stressed that while it was useful for the purposes to which it is applied, better use could be made of it. Their suggestions for how it could be improved are included under the next subsection (ways in which data considered inadequate/could be improved). The remaining three respondents highlighted the following ways in which it was useful:

- The data was adequate in clinical work with clients (but not for service planning).

- The data collected on ethnic categories informed developments related to service use by different minority groups.

- The richer data on ethnicity highlighted through interventions informed a range of areas of service development, such as staff recruitment and outreach work.

How data was considered inadequate

The ways in which data collected was said to be inadequate, relate to three main themes: consistency, information systems and client feedback.

CONSISTENCY

Greater consistency was needed:

- in the type of data collected

- data needing to be collected for all clients

- in standards of data collection within and between CAMHS teams

- across different agencies to facilitate inter-agency work.

INFORMATION SYSTEMS

Some difficulties related to how data could be collected to enable it to be used more effectively:

- A dilemma was highlighted between standardising data for the purpose of service planning which would not reflect ethnic diversity of client group and not standardising it to reflect diversity, which would not enable the collation needed for service planning.

- Qualitative data highlighted through interventions was not used to inform service developments on a regular or systematic basis due to problems of collation.

- IT systems being used did not enable more complex recording and analysis of information needed for service planning.

CLIENT FEEDBACK

More client feedback was needed in relation to their needs as well as their views about service provision. This, however, would require qualitative information and resources were not available to facilitate this.

Suggestions for improving data collection

The following suggestions were made in relation to how data collected could be improved.

- Data that is more specific about factors relating to ethnicity needs to be collected than is currently the case.

- More ethnic categories need to be used to reflect diversity, especially in relation to White European minorities.

- More relevant information needs to be available at time of referral about needs of minority groups, particularly where specialist resources such as interpreting need to be organised.

- There needs to be less reliance on ethnic identity data provided by other professionals and more on obtaining this data from clients and/or their families.

- Better IT systems are needed to facilitate collation and use of data collected.

Does the number of minority ethnic groups using the service reflect the need for it among local minority ethnic groups?

Two service managers responded that it did, five that it did not, two partly and five did not know.

The qualitative data in each of the above categories reveals that different quantitative responses can sometimes mean the same thing. For example, the issue relating to some minority ethnic groups accessing the service more than others was highlighted both by CAMHS managers who said the number of minority ethnic groups using the service *did* reflect local need, as well as those who said it *did not*.

With the exception of those who said they did not know about level of service use by minority ethnic groups, other respondents said they assessed minority ethnic groups' level of use of the service by looking at whether the percentage of minority ethnic groups using their service reflected their percentage in the local population. Though such an approach is perhaps the most practical in highlighting under- or over-representation, it does have limitations that should be borne in mind, for example:

- In the absence of appropriate epidemiological data, it is difficult to assess whether the needs of local minority ethnic groups are appropriately addressed, irrespective of their level of representation in CAMHS.

- National and local population statistics are limited in the 'ethnic' categories they use; local minority ethnic groups falling outside these categories would not be identified through such sources.

- Use of the single category 'all minority ethnic groups' would not highlight the extent to which particular minority ethnic groups were represented in the service.

These concerns were also reflected in feedback from respondents.

Minority ethnic groups using the service reflect local need

Two respondents thought the number of minority ethnic group clients using the service reflected the need for support from the service but qualified this with the following comments:

> It must be acknowledged that this is not necessarily an indication that the mental health needs of local minority ethnic groups are identified and understood.

> The overall take-up of the service reflects the overall number of minority ethnic groups in the local population; however, particular minority ethnic groups are under-represented.

Minority ethnic groups using the service do not reflect local need

The five respondents who said service use by minority ethnic groups did not reflect the need for support from the service provided valuable insights as to why they thought this was the case.

SERVICES NOT EQUIPPED TO ADDRESS THE NEEDS OF SOME MINORITY ETHNIC GROUPS

The needs of some minority ethnic groups were said to be addressed better than others. One reason given as to why the needs of some minority ethnic groups were not addressed was due to services not being sufficiently equipped to do this. For example, in relation to a lack of a) 'outreach' work to build trust and address any stigma relating to mental health; b) appropriate staffing; c) sufficient, relevant knowledge and understanding about the particular community.

LACK OF CLIENT AWARENESS AND CONFIDENCE IN THE SERVICE

Research had been commissioned by one service to obtain further information as to why the percentage of minority ethnic groups using the service was less than half their percentage in the local school population. Their study highlighted that parents were not accessing the service because there were no therapists available who spoke their language and young people were not accessing it because they had insufficient information about the service and/or concerns about confidentiality. Another respondent also highlighted stigma and concerns about confidentiality as barriers to accepting support from the service.

DISCREPANCIES BETWEEN MINORITY ETHNIC GROUPS USING THE SERVICE

One service had looked into the reasons why African Caribbean clients were over-represented in the service and South Asian clients were under-represented. In the over-represented group, young people were referred mostly by school and were on the brink of exclusion from school. The difficulties of this group were said to be perceived more readily by schools as being related to 'conduct disorder' than for other majority and minority groups. A lack of early identification and referral in this group meant that by the time young people were seen by the CAMHS, their behaviour difficulties had manifest to a high degree and their self-confidence and self-esteem were said to be quite low.

The under-represented group of South Asian clients were said to be more likely to somaticise psychological difficulties when presenting to professionals (anxiety and stress may be presented as headache or chest pains). A possible reason for the relative lack of referrals for this group could have been due to neither professional nor client being able to identify concerns as being related to mental health. The service had developed outreach work for this group and the number of referrals had started to increase since this was introduced.

LACK OF CLIENT AND PROFESSIONAL AWARENESS ABOUT MENTAL HEALTH AND CAMHS PROVISION

A lack of awareness among clients and other referrers about mental health and about what CAMHS could offer, led either to inappropriate referrals, no referrals or referrals being made too late.

LACK OF MULTIDISCIPLINARY SUPPORT IN THE SERVICE

Some CAMHS were unable to provide the range of support required from within the service (for example, social work, psychology, educational support). This posed a difficulty for some clients. Refugees were highlighted in particular, who were unable to see professionals in a range of different locations. The potential benefits of interventions that required a range of input was minimised in such situations.

WAITING LISTS

Long waiting lists were said to have an impact on all clients, including those from minority ethnic groups, resulting in non-access for varying periods of time.

Minority ethnic groups using the service partly reflect local need

Two respondents said that the number of local minority ethnic groups using the service was good for some groups, while others were under-represented and some were not represented at all.

Not known if minority ethnic groups using the service reflect local need

Five respondents said they did not know if the number of minority ethnic group clients using the service reflected local need.

> The number of minority ethnic groups using the service reflects the local minority ethnic group population, but this is not necessarily an indication that all who need support are receiving it.

> Certain groups are seen more frequently than others.

> They are probably under-represented in the service but this has not been assessed so it's difficult to say if or why this is the case. It is unclear whether this is because they don't need the service, or it's a reflection of the low number of minority ethnic groups in the local population, or whether there are other barriers.

> Information about ethnicity of clients is not recorded for about a third of the clients. In 13 per cent of these cases the clients do not wish to answer the question and in the remaining cases clinicians are not asking for this information. Also data on ethnicity is not available before the client is seen and this makes it difficult to

prepare for an appropriate intervention prior to contact with the service. This is especially serious in some circumstances such as those where an interpreter is required.

How do you ensure your staff are trained and supported to meet the needs of an ethnically diverse client group?

Training provided

Eight CAMHS teams were said to receive training related to addressing the needs of minority ethnic groups, although of these only two received this on a regular basis. The type and number of training events that staff participated in varied between teams, with some being provided with up to four training events in the previous year and others just one.

One of the eight teams was only provided with training for managers. This was mandatory training provided by the Trust on equal opportunities and covered personnel, not client, issues.

No training provided

Six respondents said that no training was provided to staff in relation to this aspect of CAMHS work. Of these, three were looking to develop this in future.

'Other' category

Qualitative responses provided under this category provide some useful insights.

- The need to provide training to interpreters was highlighted. Concerns related to the need for accurate translation and for interpreters to have an understanding of cultural as well as mental health issues.

- The availability of written materials in one service was highlighted.

- One service related that diversity and cultural awareness were a component of the service policy to provide ongoing professional development for staff.

- Difficulties in ensuring training for all staff were encountered in services that had a high turnover.

- Staff support advisors were available in one service where issues relating to ethnicity could be raised.

How do you evaluate the value of training and support provided?

A very varied picture emerged in relation to whether and how training provided was evaluated. Most teams either did not undertake formal evaluation, or completed evaluation forms that were returned to the Trust and no feedback was received by the team. A significant number of respondents did highlight informal approaches to evaluation.

Formal evaluation undertaken

Two respondents provided details of formal evaluations they undertook:

- In one team evaluation forms were given out for completion after each training event and additionally there was informal feedback between colleagues. The evaluation of training was said to indicate that whole-team training was preferred to only some members of staff participating in internal or external training events.

- The other team also used evaluation forms for each event and analysis of these indicated that training organised by the service was preferred to that organised by the Trust.

Informal evaluation only

Six respondents said there was informal evaluation only. Of these, five said this was in the form of informal feedback being shared between colleagues and one highlighted the following process:

> There is no formal evaluation. Feedback about training is given during individual supervision as well as between colleagues. Staff support needs should be addressed through individual supervision and individual action plans.

Evaluation forms completed for the health authority or Trust

Four respondents said evaluation forms were completed and sent to the Trust but the teams received no feedback.

No evaluation undertaken

Two respondents said no evaluation was undertaken. One of these related that a one-off study had been commissioned and completed two years previously which highlighted what was working and where the gaps were in relation to staff training.

Difficulties in relation to evaluation

In one team evaluation forms had been completed in the past but were not found to be useful; as a result the team now shared informal feedback only.

Another respondent thought it would be impossible to evaluate all training because the time and resources needed for this were not available.

Does your team include staff from minority ethnic groups?

Eleven of 13 teams had staff from minority ethnic groups on their team in clinical, managerial and administrative positions. Only one team had no staff from minority ethnic groups and two teams had clinicians only of minority ethnic origin.

Three of the respondents who said the team had staff occupying all positions said they needed more staff from minority ethnic groups. One respondent who did not know said this was because the number of staff and positions they occupied changed all the time due to high turnover. An important issue was highlighted by the respondent who said there were no staff from minority ethnic groups on the team:

> It has been difficult to recruit staff from minority ethnic groups with relevant training and especially difficult to get such staff from a cross section of disciplines such as social work, psychiatry and psychology. The Trust is now considering recruiting staff from minority ethnic groups as trainees and supporting their training.

Do you think your staff would benefit from additional training in this area?

With the exception of two CAMHS managers who did not know whether staff would benefit from additional training, the 12 others were of the opinion that staff would benefit from further training in relation to meeting the needs of minority ethnic groups.

Asked what training format would be most useful, those who thought staff would benefit from further training suggested a range of formats as being potentially useful. Their responses are summarised in Table II.5 and detailed feedback follows.

Table II.5 What training format would be most useful?	
Team-based training	3
Participation in local training events	3
Combination as relevant including national events	5
Other	3

Team-based training

Those suggesting team-based training were of the opinion that it was important that the whole staff team had access to learning. Situations in which only some staff had participated in training were said to have resulted in the ideas they brought back for the service not being received with equal enthusiasm by colleagues who had not participated. Team training was considered valuable for team-building purposes to facilitate whole-team knowledge, understanding and motivation for change.

Local training events

Respondents citing local training thought these would be useful for addressing issues that were specific to the context of local communities.

Combination of training, including national training events

A combination of training relevant to staff needs were favoured by some respondents who made the following points:

- Teams are likely to be comprised of staff whose individual training needs are different from each other. Training events would need to take this into account to maximise their benefit.

- Access to written resources – before, during and after training as relevant – was considered useful.

- There was a need in some teams to first raise team awareness about issues relating to the mental health of minority ethnic groups. Other, more specific areas for training would be highlighted through this exercise.

- Participation in national events (including conferences) was considered important in order to obtain a wider picture and understanding.

- Access to people with relevant expertise, to discuss issues as they arose, was considered to be a useful approach to acquiring relevant knowledge.

Other training

Other suggestions in relation to the format for training included:

- Having written resources available in the service for reference purposes.

- An ongoing programme of training would be most useful (as opposed to one-off events).

- A lack of time and other resources resulted in some staff having to 'learn on the job'. Consideration was needed about how training needs could be addressed in such circumstances.

Particular training needs

Four respondents highlighted the need for an analysis of staff training needs in order to identify and prioritise areas in which training would be useful. The remaining respondents highlighted a number of subject areas that can be divided into those that are of a general nature and those that are more specific.

GENERAL AREAS OF TRAINING

- The experiences of children from (minority ethnic group) households that have different beliefs and practices to their majority counterparts

- the needs of local minority ethnic groups under-represented in the service

- developing sensitivity to other cultures

- perceptions of mental illness in different cultures
- enabling staff to express attitudes relating to ethnicity which some staff may be unwilling to express (which can be a necessary precursor if more specific areas of training relating to CAMHS for minority ethnic groups are to be effective)
- factors relevant to access and appropriateness of services.

SPECIFIC AREAS OF TRAINING

- Issues relevant to translation and interpreting
- the impact of child care legislation in a multi-ethnic context
- recruitment of staff from minority ethnic groups
- post-traumatic stress
- issues relating to the matching of clinician and client in consultation
- ethnicity and the mental health needs of children looked after.

Do you use targeted publicity to inform minority ethnic groups about your services?

No targeted publicity

Eleven of the 14 CAMHS managers said none was undertaken though the responses indicated that most services recognise the need for this. A range of reasons were cited as to why targeted publicity was not being undertaken:

ISSUE BEING CONSIDERED FOR FUTURE DEVELOPMENT

The information needs of all clients were being reviewed in one service and the needs of minority ethnic groups were being considered as part of this overall review. Another service was undertaking research to look at minority ethnic groups' views about CAMHS; ways to address their information needs would be considered after the research was completed.

THE INFORMATION NEEDS OF ALL CLIENTS NOT ADDRESSED

Three respondents highlighted that services were not addressing this for any client groups and that it needed to be prioritised both at a general level and for specific groups such as minority ethnic groups.

THE NEED TO ALLOCATE RESPONSIBILITY FOR TAKING THIS FORWARD

One service related that specific targeting of information to minority ethnic groups did take place in another area covered by the Trust, which had a specialist group set up to provide counselling to minority ethnic groups. The service in which the survey respondent was based did not have a similar specialist group and that contributed to there being a lack of similar targeting in the service.

SERVICES NOT PREPARED FOR ACCEPTING SELF-REFERRALS

Two respondents related that their service only accepted referrals from other agencies and professionals. Consequently, it would be inappropriate to publicise the service directly to potential clients (including those from minority ethnic groups) if self-referrals were not accepted. Both felt that input provided by the service to other initiatives (such as parenting programmes) that were working with minority ethnic groups would raise awareness among participants of those groups about CAMHS provision.

LACK OF RESOURCES

A lack of funding for publicity purposes was cited as an obstacle.

Publicity material provided outside of a targeted approach

Leaflets translated in other languages were made available by some services and it was recognised that this was not a targeted approach. This is illustrated in the following comments:

> Leaflets are provided in the waiting room in English and one other language. Other than this it is difficult to know why there is no targeted publicity.

> Some of the general publicity leaflets may be available in other languages, but nothing more than this is done and it is certainly not targeted.

Targeted publicity undertaken

The three services that did undertake targeted publicity provided valuable insights into approaches that can inform this work. The need for more than one approach is apparent in their feedback:

Through targeted informing of professionals and voluntary sector groups working with local communities and by printing information leaflets in a number of languages.

Members of the team attend events organised by and for minority ethnic groups at local venues, such as the Hindu temple. A stall is set up and staff are at hand to talk and answer questions. We are also currently considering the translation of written information into different languages.

Relevant voluntary organisations (working with minority communities) are invited to exchange information with the service about what each other does and look at ways of working together. Information about the service is made available in different languages.

Do you feel your service is able to meet the needs of an ethnically and culturally diverse population?

Table II.6 Meeting the population's needs			
Yes	No	Partly	Don't know
2	3	8	1

The majority of services said that this was achieved partly.

Needs of a culturally diverse population met

The feedback from the two respondents who said 'Yes' demonstrates differences in criteria for assessing whether services meet the needs of a culturally diverse client group, as well as in approaches that facilitate the work to be undertaken.

By setting up specialist services such as the Refugee Project and by collaborating with other services that have the relevant expertise.

This response highlights a limited number of approaches when compared to the following:

In a number of ways:

- By working through GP surgeries.

- Providing drop-in surgeries in schools one day a week.

- Some of the young people identified through GP surgeries and schools may then be referred on to the Tier 3 service.

- Developing outreach projects (with specialist funding) targeted at particular groups that would include minority ethnic groups. For example, youth groups or to tackle social exclusion.

- Establishing links with front line professionals such as health visitors to facilitate understanding between professionals and provide input to clients at Tiers 1 and 2 if necessary.

Factors that facilitate or hinder meeting the needs of culturally diverse client groups

Data from respondents can be summarised as factors said to facilitate or hinder meeting the needs of a culturally diverse client group.

FACTORS THAT FACILITATE

- Developing specialist services aimed at particular minority groups

- collaborating with other agencies that have relevant expertise

- flexibility in service provision – for example, undertaking outreach work, drop-in surgeries at GP clinics and schools, home visits, working with community groups

- regular links with front line staff at Tiers 1 and 2 to facilitate understanding of roles and provide input to clients if necessary

- access to good interpreting services

- developing the role of interpreters as co-workers in the service

- experienced and culturally competent staff

- a culturally diverse staff team.

Not surprisingly, factors highlighted as hindering the provision of services to meet the needs of a culturally diverse client group were mostly the opposite of those said to facilitate such provision.

FACTORS THAT HINDER

- Lack of funding to develop or sustain specialist services and approaches
- lack of resources to access interpreting services
- lack of access to good quality interpreting
- lack of a culturally diverse staff team
- lack of cultural competence in the service
- lack of culturally competent training across mental health disciplines
- inadequate information systems
- restructuring of services – resulting in the needs of minority groups not being prioritised.

Have you evaluated the impact of services provided for minority ethnic groups?

Nine of the 14 CAMHS did not evaluate the impact of provision to minority ethnic groups. The three services that did and the two that partly did, either evaluated this aspect of the work as part of wider service evaluation or only evaluated initiatives targeted specifically at minority ethnic groups.

Evaluation undertaken

Two approaches were highlighted by respondents saying they evaluated the impact of provision to minority ethnic groups.

- One service administered a client satisfaction questionnaire to all clients; feedback provided by clients from minority ethnic groups was given specific consideration. This service was also in the process of introducing a new system of 'before and after' (the intervention) evaluation.

- Two respondents said all clients were asked for feedback on a regular basis in relation to various aspects of the service and the needs of minority ethnic groups were considered within this. One of these services had also commissioned a detailed one-off study of an initiative it set up to address the needs of local minority ethnic groups.

Evaluation partly undertaken

Those who said provision to minority ethnic groups was partly evaluated communicated that this was done only in relation to provision that was targeted specifically at minority ethnic groups.

> Projects developed specifically to work with young people from minority ethnic groups have ongoing evaluation as part of the programme of work. No other impact is evaluated.

> The project developed for minority ethnic groups has ongoing evaluation. Outcomes of interventions are evaluated generally but not broken down by ethnicity, though the service has clients from minority ethnic groups.

Evaluation not undertaken

Those saying that services did not evaluate provision to minority ethnic groups highlighted obstacles relating to evaluation tools, information systems, lack of resources or simply that this was not done. Some were considering how this aspect of the work could be developed in future.

NEED FOR APPROPRIATE RESOURCES AND EVALUATION TOOLS

> To date there have been insufficient resources to enable the development of tools that would facilitate this. However, the Trust is keen to develop this for the future.

INFORMATION SYSTEMS

> Evaluation is not currently undertaken generally but the service is in the process of setting up information systems to enable this. Ethnicity could be a part of this (what is evaluated).

> The impact of individual clinical interventions is assessed by the clinicians but this information is not collated/analysed. This is currently being discussed with the Trust IT department to look at developing systems that could facilitate this in future.

IRREGULAR APPROACHES LACKING A FOCUS ON ETHNICITY

> Occasional audits are undertaken to look at customer satisfaction but this is not done regularly or broken down by ethnicity.

Do clients from minority ethnic groups contribute to any aspect of planning and provision of services?

Minority ethnic communities are often under-represented in decision-making positions and their involvement in needs assessments as well as policy and planning decisions is important (Bhui, Christie and Bhugra 1995; Hardman and Harris 1998; Rawaf 1998). Services need to adopt a client-led approach and not be based on professional assumptions about what clients need.

Clients from minority ethnic groups did not contribute to planning provision in ten of the 14 CAMHS, only two respondents said that clients contributed and a further two that they contributed partly. Where clients from minority ethnic groups did contribute, this was as part of contributions provided by all clients. The relative merits and drawbacks of this were not explored in this survey.

Approaches to facilitate client contribution

The two respondents who said clients contributed highlighted the following approaches to their involvement:

- In one service client feedback, including clients from minority ethnic groups, on various aspects of service provision was said to be obtained regularly, discussed regularly at team meetings and incorporated in service development/change wherever possible. In this service, one example of how client feedback led to change in the service was in relation to the decor to make it more reflective of the various community groups that attended the clinic.

- Another service highlighted three ways in which clients contributed:

  - 1. Through a 'user group', which included clients from minority ethnic groups and which met regularly with clinicians to give feedback about different aspects of the service.

  - 2. Clients were also given forms to complete which asked for their feedback about what they liked and disliked about the service.

     ○   3. The views from both the above approaches were presented at team meetings and possibilities for improvement/development were discussed.

Respondents saying that clients from minority ethnic groups contributed 'partly' to planning provision said this was either because they only contributed to some aspects of provision or their feedback had not yet been used.

> Clients (including those from minority ethnic groups) contribute to initiatives that CAMHS works on in partnership with others, e.g. Neighbourhood Renewal. Other than this there is no involvement in planning CAMHS provision.

> A survey has been conducted to get feedback from clients (including minority ethnic groups) but no other involvement has taken place to date.

Reasons given for no client contribution

The following reasons were given by respondents who said there was no contribution from minority ethnic group clients to planning provision of services.

A NEED TO DEVELOP CLIENT CONTRIBUTIONS GENERALLY

Nine respondents said this area needed to be developed for all CAMHS clients in the future. Participation of minority ethnic group clients would be considered as part of this overall development. Such developments were already under way in two services which were in the process of recruiting clients, including minority ethnic group clients, to join 'user' forums.

THE NEED TO AVOID TOKEN INVOLVEMENT

One respondent highlighted the difficulty in negotiating a culturally diverse client group so that they were usefully involved without their contributions becoming a token gesture.

Do you liaise with other agencies who have relevant expertise in this field?

All except two CAMHS managers said they liaised with other agencies that had relevant expertise in relation to addressing the needs of minority ethnic groups. Respondents for the two services that did not liaise with other agencies said they would like to develop contacts in future.

The most frequent contact was with a combination of voluntary/community and statutory sector services (seven respondents), followed by voluntary and community sector only (three respondents), voluntary/community and private (two respondents) and statutory sector only (one respondent).

The nature of contact with the various agencies is summarised in Table II.7.

Table II.7 Sector in which liaison agencies were based					
Nature of contact with other agencies	Vol/Com only	Vol/Com & Private	Vol/Com & Statut	Statut only	No contact
Make and receive referrals	2		4	1	
Make referrals only			1v		
Receive referrals only			1v		
Joint training	1		2		
Joint work with clients	2		3	1	
Access specialist input for client		2			
Share knowledge and information			4	1	
Outreach work		1	2		
Interpreting		2			
Agency facilitates group work	1				
Need to develop contact in future					2

Key: v = Type of contact with the voluntary/community agencies only

Table II.7 indicates contact with agencies across the voluntary and community, private and statutory sectors. The voluntary and community sector features very prominently. The nature of contact varies, some being client-focused (e.g. outreach work) while other contact is more service-focused (e.g. joint training).

Some key themes relating to the provision of services by the voluntary sector are highlighted in Appendix 1.

References

Bahl, V. (1998) 'Ethnic minority groups: national perspective.' In S. Rawaf and V. Bahl (eds) *Assessing health needs of people from minority ethnic groups.* pp.3–21. London: Royal College of Physicians.

Bhui, K., Christie, Y. and Bhugra, D. (1995) 'The essential elements of culturally sensitive psychiatric services.' *International Journal of Social Psychiatry 41*, 242–256.

Chandra, J. (1996) *Facing up to difference: a toolkit for creating culturally competent health services for black and minority ethnic communities.* London: King's Fund.

Hardman, E. and Harris, R. (1998) *Developing and evaluating community mental health services: Volume 1, The Bangladeshi community, assessment of need.* London: Tavistock Clinic.

House of Commons Health Committee (1997) *Child and Adolescent Mental Health Services. Health Committee Fourth Report: Session 1996–97, HC 26-I.* London: HMSO.

Kurtz, Z., Thornes, R. and Wolkind, S. (1994) *Services for the mental health of children and young people in England: A national review.* London: South West Thames Regional Health Authority and Department of Health.

Malek, M. (1997) *Nurturing Healthy Minds – the Importance of the Voluntary Sector in the Promoting Young People's Mental Health.* London: National Children's Bureau.

Rawaf, S. (1998) 'Theoretical Framework.' In S. Rawaf and V. Bahl (eds) *Assessing health needs of people from minority ethnic groups.* pp.21–35. London: Royal College of Physicians.

Singh, J. (1998) *Developing the role of the black and minority ethnic voluntary sector in a changing NHS.* London: Department of Health.

Voluntary Sector Involvement

FOCUS seminar

In September 2001 FOCUS invited a range of representatives from the voluntary sector to a seminar. We wanted to gain further insights into the following areas:

- participants' views about why they thought clients used voluntary services instead of, or in addition to, those provided by the statutory sector

- the ways in which participants thought voluntary sector services were similar to, or different from, those provided through the statutory sector

- the nature of links and partnerships with services in the statutory sector

- the extent to which participants thought statutory services in their locality were able to address the needs of young people from minority ethnic groups – that is, to highlight what worked and identify any gaps.

The themes highlighted reflect many of the issues highlighted in available literature and through the FOCUS survey. What follows is a short description of the four projects participating in the seminar, followed by an account of the main themes emerging from presentations and discussion.

Seminar participants

Trinity Community Centre

This Centre was established in 1972 by local residents in Newham, East London, to meet the needs of local people living in one of London's poorest boroughs. The Centre aims to support and empower people who feel marginalised and to improve the conditions of life for people using its services. The cultural diversity of the area is reflected in the Centre with people of 63 different nationalities using its services. A variety of activities are provided, with 62 activity groups using the Centre which caters for a range of age groups and needs. Of particular relevance to the seminar was the Centre's work with unaccompanied young refugees.

East Birmingham Family Service Unit

This project is part of a national network of Family Service Units, which became a national charity in the 1950s. Individual units are located in the communities they serve and aim to address socio-economic deprivation through a combination of practical and emotional support. This particular unit is based in an area of high socio-economic deprivation and the local community is comprised mostly of Pakistani and Bangladeshi families and a significant Yemeni population. A range of social work, group work, parenting advice and other support is offered and the service also undertakes work on behalf of statutory services.

Confederation of Indian Organisations

This organisation was established as a charity in 1975 to support South Asian voluntary organisations nationally. It undertakes a range of work to support other organisations, commissions relevant research, holds conferences and seminars as well as providing direct support to clients. A number if its publications have focused on health and mental health of South Asian communities and the organisation has a mental health team, of two staff, which provides a counselling and befriending service to South Asian women aged 15 years and over. A number of the women to whom support is provided have children and where appropriate, the team supports the women to address issues concerning their children.

Themes relevant to work with minority ethnic groups highlighted in the seminar

Through presentations and discussion, participants highlighted a number of aspects that appear to be effective in working with clients from minority ethnic groups. Issues relating to the interface between statutory and voluntary sector provision were also discussed.

Physical space of a service

Physical design of the building makes an important contribution to client accessibility. The space should look and feel inviting, a factor often overlooked or not given due prominence by agencies.

Refugee children and young people 'looked after'

Unaccompanied young refugees attending the Trinity Centre are usually adolescents with little or no structures, boundaries or rules in their lives. Being in the social services 'looked after' system can sometimes exacerbate this. Some of the reasons for this and approaches to addressing concerns were highlighted as follows.

Standards of care for young people 'looked after' vary and in children's homes this can result in the young person not receiving sufficient supervision. In the case of unaccompanied minors who are placed in out-of-borough accommodation, they may not have sufficient contact with the social worker to facilitate regular supervision. Social work carers of the young people are often highly committed but can have limited training in working with this particular group. Where there is a high turnover of staff this can result in a lack of consistency in relation to the adults whom children relate to. Such situations do not facilitate the building of trusting relationships. The Trinity Centre aims to support the young people to build friendships and contacts, which is achieved through day-to-day work as well as residential courses.

Given the traumatic experiences many of these children have had, they often do not respond to formal counselling but open up to staff at the Centre with whom they have built a trusting relationship. Another route for expressing emotions is provided through creative activities such as the visual and performing arts. In a recent initiative, the children made a short film and this provided a focus and structure; the value of such approaches should not be underestimated.

The time it takes for a young person to talk about their concerns varies and depends on their individual circumstances. A significant point appears to be when they realise the project is there to help them. For example, one client was greatly concerned about being moved to supported accommodation from a children's home which would have left him living on his own without the support and company of his housemates. He did not speak about these concerns until he realised the role of the advocacy service at the Centre was to help him to address such issues. Once young people realise the role of services, it seems easier for them to voice issues and ask for support.

Working with families from diverse ethnic backgrounds

Language was emphasised as an important factor in enabling families to access services and support. The Family Service Unit is able to offer services in a range of languages. This is recognised by the local social services department which funds the Unit to undertake work with families in a first language.

The issue of how language may affect access is also demonstrated by the fact that the Unit had little contact with the local Yemeni community until an Arabic-speaking worker was appointed. Since this appointment the numbers accessing support from this community has increased.

Other features that are considered by the Unit to be valuable in working with families of minority ethnic origin include:

- The Unit does not have the power to remove children into care. Families who are reluctant to use services due to a fear of their children being taken away, appear to be more comfortable using provision such as that available at the Unit.

- The Unit is able to offer long-term support and this appears to be valued by clients. Staff from the Unit befriending scheme are able to take up work with families where statutory input, from social services for example, has ended but support is still needed. Befrienders maintain support and contact even when there is no specific 'task'. They will also help with things like accompanying clients to other agencies such as housing and welfare support. This helps to build trust and sustain a supportive network.

Reasons why clients value support from voluntary sector services
FLEXIBILITY

At the Trinity Centre staff respond to children's needs as they arise. The way statutory services are structured may not facilitate addressing needs that do not fit in to the way existing provision is delivered. Another factor is that unaccompanied minors are a relatively new phenomenon in the locality and cannot be dealt with effectively within existing structures of statutory services.

Although a structured service is not always on offer at Trinity, the young people see it as a 'safe' place which they can use to access various types of support and recreational activities and they know the staff. The children know that whenever they turn up, they can be seen and helped. This sort of service cannot be accessed in the statutory sector. Long-term, 'as and when' help is what is provided at the Centre and is what is required by the children. The statutory sector does not work in this way.

PAST EXPERIENCE OF STATUTORY PROVISION

Many of the families attending the Family Service Unit appear to have had negative experiences with statutory services in the past. Those highlighted include poor diagnosis by services, communication problems relating to cultural and/or language issues and difficulties in monitoring treatment. Other factors that may prevent use of statutory provision by clients at the Unit include:

- community or cultural pressures, such as the shame attached to accessing support
- lack of awareness about available services and in recognising difficulties
- lack of availability of appropriate language/translation facilities.

Knowledge about the community

The Family Service Unit was said to have significant knowledge about the local community that statutory services may not. For example, it was aware that:

- Bangladeshi children in the community are the highest risk group for school exclusion. The Unit believes this is linked to institutional racism in schools which affects children's behaviour, placing them at risk of exclusion.
- Domestic violence is a significant concern in the local community.
- Some women do not leave home unescorted which has implications for children and in accessing services.
- There are generational issues in some families relating to differences in opinion about appropriate behaviour and cultural

norms. This can leave some children to deal with the conflicts arising from this.

- There is an 80 per cent illiteracy rate among the Yemeni population in the area. This presents a problem for the children in their schooling.

- Individuals from dual heritage homes are exposed to a significant amount of racism.

- Young mothers who are socially isolated often present with low self-esteem.

Few local statutory services are likely to have this depth of knowledge about the community.

Based in the community

The voluntary sector was said to have success in reaching clients because of the way it works. It is important to recognise that services in the statutory sector can be physically and geographically 'removed' from people. Community services need to be in the community. Networking is very important to identify what people want in the changing profile of minority ethnic communities.

Families may not access services just because they know the services are there. Much health education work needs to be done. Building a trusting relationship with local communities can facilitate referrals by one service to another. Clients may come in for support for a particular issue and can be helped to access other services, such as housing or help with domestic violence. Adolescents do not often go straight to adolescent mental health services but rather access them via services such as those in the voluntary sector.

Working with statutory services

Participants felt that services in statutory and voluntary sectors needed to work together and to have some knowledge of the types of services each provided. Effective collaboration was said to enhance the type of support provided, particularly when the amount and type of child and adolescent mental health provision in the statutory sector was limited.

The Family Service Unit highlighted that it was often commissioned by local social services to carry out child protection assessments with families whom social services were not able to assess themselves. Here, a voluntary sector service was said to be able to engage families in a way the statutory sector could not. It was important to look at why the voluntary sector was able to achieve this. Furthermore, this sector was said to work not just with minority ethnic groups but had success in engaging majority groups as well. This was said to emphasise the need to look at those features that contribute to achieving success in engaging clients.

The statutory sector was also recognised as providing support to voluntary agencies and effective links could speed up the process of providing relevant interventions to clients.

For example, the Trinity Centre would value support from a psychologist or psychiatrist in addressing trauma and behavioural issues. This would require professionals to work with the clients in a way they would find to be 'non-threatening'.

A high staff turnover was said to result in weakening voluntary/statutory links because of the need to constantly establish working relationships with new staff.

Voluntary sector links with CAMHS

Representatives from the voluntary sector largely referred to social services and education establishments in relation to links with the statutory sector. Asked why they had not referred to CAMHS services, it emerged that they in fact had very few links with CAMHS and highlighted the following reasons:

- Long waiting lists did not facilitate referral of clients.

- Being located a considerable geographical distance from the community also did not facilitate referrals or planning collaborative work.

- Often the specialist services such as CAMHS were only able to accept referrals of children who had reached crisis point.

- Some CAMHS would not accept clients if they felt the home situation was not sufficiently settled to provide counselling.

- Clients often needed weekly support and CAMHS could only offer less frequent support.

- Voluntary projects found it difficult to access a number of statutory services but felt this was more so with CAMHS.

- CAMHS were not always set up to provide culturally sensitive services and staff from voluntary sector services would be reluctant to refer clients unless they had some assurance that cultural sensitivity would be addressed. In the absence of cultural sensitivity, voluntary sector services were more likely to seek specialist support for clients from another voluntary sector agency.

- Voluntary sector services were said to deal with mental health as one of a number of issues and saw mental health issues in a holistic fashion. This made it difficult to work with CAMHS if they adopted a different approach that was less holistic.

- CAMHS services were seen largely to rely on referrals being made to them. A more productive approach would be to undertake outreach work and accept self-referrals.

- There was often no 'direct line' to CAMHS, so it was necessary to go through the GP or the social services department and this approach was not helpful.

Funding

In addition to the insecurity created by short-term funding arrangements, a number of other issues were highlighted in relation to funding work with minority ethnic groups in both statutory and voluntary sectors.

Statutory services were said to encounter difficulties in securing funding for specialist work. For example, the Marlborough Family Service (see Appendix II) had support from senior management in securing funding for the development of specialist work with minority ethnic groups. Though the initiatives were proposed from within the statutory sector, there was some debate as to whether the work was to be funded from within the statutory sector. It was, ultimately, funded and run by the statutory sector. However, had statutory funding not been forthcoming the service would have applied for voluntary sector funding. Support from management at a senior level was highlighted as an important component in establishing and sustaining specialist provision.

Much innovative work was said to be lost in the voluntary sector when funding was only available for a fixed period. The funding period was said to usually come to an end just as projects had developed sufficiently and 'found their feet'. This was said to be a difficulty that had particular implications for minority ethnic groups, because many of the services they use appear to be located in the voluntary sector.

Quantifying the nature of support that enabled access to funding was also said to be difficult. For example, young people at the Trinity Centre were often supported to acquire basic cooking and housekeeping skills to help them move from social services accommodation to independent living. This support and training was seen as vital but it was also hard to quantify its value, which in turn made it difficult to develop funding bids for such work.

Another difficulty in relation to quantifying support was the time taken to build trust and carefully negotiate family involvement, especially with families who already had a mistrust of services. A lot of time and other resources could be spent travelling to see people and funders did not always understand or see the value of this approach.

The move towards evidence-based work was seen as potentially creating further difficulties in securing funding for work that could not be quantified. For example, the success of the 'feel good' factor was a difficult one to measure but often an essential aspect of effectively engaging clients. Such qualitative factors could not be easily described and affected funding.

The need to recognise and involve the voluntary sector as a key player

Though this seminar was a relatively small event it has nevertheless high-lighted some very important issues and concerns about addressing the needs of minority ethnic groups. Many of these have been highlighted in other texts which recognise the value of developing collaborative approaches with this sector in all aspects of planning and service delivery.

Examples of Projects/Services

The Multi-Agency Preventative Project (MAP)
1 Ewart Place
Gladstone Place
London E3 5EQ
Tel: 0207 364 2097/2185
Fax: 0207 364 2161
Email: maswood.ahmed@towerhamlets.gov.uk

MAP is a joint enterprise between Tower Hamlets Social Services Department, Education, East London and City Mental Health NHS Health Trust, the Youth Service (Tower Hamlets) and the voluntary sector.

The project aims to:

1. Offer an early preventative intervention service to adolescent Bangladeshi boys and their families.
2. Support boys at risk of or experiencing emotional difficulties which prevent them from making the best of schools and their social surroundings.
3. Offer a culturally appropriate service, which is accessible to both adolescent Bangladeshi boys and their families.

Marlborough Family Service
38 Marlborough Place
St John's Wood
London NW8 0PJ
Tel: 020 7624 8605
Fax: 020 7328 2185
Email: mfs@cnwl.nhs.uk

This is a statutory mental health service based in the Westminster and Kensington & Chelsea Health Care Trust, an area that has a population from diverse ethnic groups and includes areas of extreme wealth as well as extreme poverty. An all-age referral service, it is staffed by a multidisciplinary team and incorporates a CAMHS. The range of services offered include support on an individual basis, a Family Day Unit and an Education Unit where school-age children requiring intensive support attend a classroom setting with family members. Staff are also available for consultation and training to other professionals. Recognising that clients and staff from minority ethnic groups were under-represented in the service and the need for it to address issues relating to racism and culture, a specialist training course was set up in 1986. Subsequently a number of specialist projects aimed at addressing the needs of minority ethnic groups have been developed and the number of clients from minority ethnic groups using the service has increased. Within the Marlborough Family Service is the Asian Counselling Service which works closely with the voluntary sector.

Young Refugees' Mental Health Service

St Mary's Department of Child and Adolescent Psychiatry
17 Paddington Green
London W2 1LQ
Tel: 020 7723 1081
Fax: 020 7723 1926

This service was established in 1996 in a primary school in North Westminster, and has expanded since then to other schools and Bayswater Family Centre (voluntary sector service for homeless families). The aims of the service continue to be the reduction of psychological distress and social impairment in young asylum seekers and refugees. This is achieved by working with community institutions that have contact with many young refugees, such as local schools and the City of Westminster Department of Social Services, Children and Families Section. Child and adolescent mental health professionals such as family therapists and psychologists are recruited to the service to work with teachers and others to provide consultation, treatment in community settings and also support referral of more impaired children to Tier 3 settings. The service is linked to the Tier 3 clinic St Mary's Department of Child and Adolescent Psychiatry, at Paddington Green, London and is situated within CNWL Mental Health Trust. The NHS and the charity Action for Children in Conflict financially support the service. The service is evaluated and more detailed accounts are available in the following publications.

O'Shea, B., Hodes, M., Down, G. and Bramley, J. (2000) 'A school-based mental health service for refugee children.' *Clinical Child Psychology and Psychiatry 5*, 189–201.

Hodes, M. (2002) 'Implications for psychiatric services of chronic civilian strife or war: young refugees in the UK.' *Advances in Psychiatric Treatment 8*, 366–374.

Mental Health Outreach for Ethnic Minority Children in Northampton

Northampton Child, Adolescent and Family Services
8 Notre Dame Mews
Northampton NN1 2BG
Tel: 01604 604608

This project aims to:

1. Develop outreach community support to ethnic minority families in relation to their children's mental health (as a Tier 1 activity).
2. Inform and facilitate access to services at higher tiers.
3. Inform professionals at higher tiers about child mental health needs of ethnic minority families and about culturally sensitive therapeutic interventions.

The project to date has:

1. Established a communication network and important community contacts.
2. Organised mental health events for different ethnic minority communities.
3. Provided consultation, liaison and support to other services and agencies.
4. Within the child and family service improved staff awareness and made the service more welcoming to ethnic minority groups.

Building Bridges Project

13 Croxteth Road
Liverpool L8 3SE
Tel: 0151 726 1893

The Building Bridges Project is a Health Action Zone Innovation Project managed by Royal Liverpool Children's NHS Trust. This is a community-based project that aims to develop and improve services for Black and minority ethnic/racial children and their families. The focus is on the psychological and emotional well-being of families, and the project offers short-term counselling, support, advice, help with using other services, and sensitivity to racial, cultural and religious issues.

Coram Leaving Care Service (CLCS)

5 Rochester Road
London NW1 9JH
Tel: 020 7267 9369
Fax: 020 7267 6944
Email: manager4@coram.org.uk
Web site: www.coram.org.uk/services/leaving.htm

CLCS provides a range of support services for young men leaving care. Their boys2MEN (b2M) Project is an innovative group work programme for looked after Black young men and is developing a self-esteem programme for young offenders. The project teaches boys and young men how to be in touch with their own feelings and have greater regard for the feelings of others. The techniques used include music, education and group work.

Antenna Outreach Service

9 Bruce Grove
Tottenham
London N17 6RA
Tel: 020 8365 9537
Email: info@antennaoutreach.co.uk

This is a mental health project for young Black African and African Caribbean people. The service is aimed at young people who have dropped out of education and employment and who regularly miss fixed appointments, or who have a history of non-compliance with medication, excessive use of recreational drugs or alcohol, or owing to their chaotic lifestyle have been identified as being at risk to themselves or others. The service also offers practical and emotional support to parents and carers.

Servol Community Trust

9 Trinity Road
London SW17 7SD
Tel: 020 8767 9650
Fax: 020 8767 9650

This provides a counselling service and information about the mental health needs of Black and ethnic communities.

Merton Oasis Project

Suite No 2
Ground Floor Justin Plaza
Mitcham
Surrey CR4 4BE
Tel: 020 8255 4033

The Merton Oasis Project aims to improve mental health services in Merton for people from the African Caribbean and Asian communities by assisting them to access mainstream services and through the provision of alternative services.

Keighley Asian Women's and Children's Centre

Eastwood Centre
Marlborough Street
Keighley
West Yorkshire BD21 3HU
Tel: 01535 667 359

This is a child care-based family centre offering private nursery for pre-school children, advice, counselling and support, language, literacy and numeracy training for local Asian women, creche facilities and evening classes for children 8+ years in Bangladeshi and Urdu, a girls' group (13+), classes for children generally 8–15 years, job search and careers advice for young women, and homework club.

The Forward Project

Windmill Lodge
Uxbridge Road
Southall UB1 3EU
Tel: 020 8578 1567

The Forward Project provides free individual psychotherapy and counselling for people of African, Caribbean and Asian descent who are suffering from mental illness or are assessed as in need of such a service. There are also psychotherapy groups.

Asian Family Counselling Service

Suite 51 The Lodge
2–4 Windmill Lane
Southall
Middlesex UB2 4NJ
Tel: 020 8571 3933
Fax: 020 8571 3933
Email: afcs99@hotmail.com

This is a private service providing crisis counselling and marriage counselling to members of the Asian community. There is also a mental health support group for women available.

Resources and Organisations

Books and publications:

In Safe Hands: a resource and training pack to support work with young refugee children. **Save the Children (2001).**
ISBN 1 84187 0390
Price £20.00
Save the Children Publications
C/o Plymbridge Distributors Ltd.
Estover Road
Plymouth PL6 7PY
Email: orders@plymbridge.com
Web site: www.savethechildren.org.uk

Klimidis, S. and Gordon, A. (1999) *Bibliography of Multi-lingual Mental Heath Assessment Instruments.* **Melbourne: Victoria Transcultural Psychiatry Unit.**
ABN 49 871 843 475
$20.00 (Australian Dollars, plus postage and packing)
Victorian Transcultural Psychiatry Unit
Level 2, Bolte Wing
St Vincent's Hospital
Nicholson Street
Fitzroy
Victoria 3065
Australia
Email: info@vtpu.org.au

Web-based resources:

Queensland Health Guides to Culturally Sensitive Health Provision
www.health.qld.gov.au/multicultural/cultdiv/default.asp

Resources include guidelines to practice, checklists for cultural assessments and guide to working with interpreters.

Multicultural Mental Health Australia
http://www.mmha.org.au

Resources include cultural awareness checklists, publications and translated patient information.

Organisations:

MIND
15–19 Broadway
London E15 4BQ
Tel: 020 8519 2122
Email: contact@mind.org.uk
Web site: www.mind.org.uk

A range of factsheets are available online, which cover issues relating to the mental health of minority ethnic groups.

Joseph Rowntree Foundation (JRF)
The Homestead
40 Water End
York
North Yorkshire YO30 6WP
Tel: 01904 629 241
Email: info@jrf.org.uk
Web site: www.jrf.org.uk

The JRF produce a range of online 'findings' from their research programme. Topics covered include care management and assessment from an anti-racist perspective, and meeting the needs of refugee families and their children.

The Institute for Race Relations

2–6 Leeke Street
London
WC1X 9HS
Tel: 020 7837 0041 / 020 7833 2010
Email: info@irr.org.uk
Web site: www.irr.org.uk

The Institute for Race Relations was established in 1958 as an independent educational charity. It aims to promote the study of race relations and make suggestions for their improvement. The web site provides a range of information of initiatives such as Home Beats (a project using multimedia technology for anti-racist education) to raise self-esteem and identity in young Black children.

Centre for Evidence on Ethnicity, Health and Diversity (CEEHD)

Centre for Health Services Studies
University of Warwick
Coventry CV4 7AL
Tel: 024 7652 3985
Web site: http://users.wbs.ac.uk/group/ceehd

CEEHD aims to ensure that available research evidence contributes to the development of effective and efficient policies and practices in ethnicity and health.

The Commission for Racial Equality (CRE)

St Dunstan's House
201–211 Borough High Street
London SE1 1GZ
Tel: 020 7939 0000
Email: info@cre.gov.uk
Web site: www.cre.gov.uk

The CRE is a publicly funded, non-governmental body set up under the Race Relations Act 1976 to tackle racial discrimination and promote racial equality. It works with public bodies, businesses and organisations from all sectors to promote policies and practices that will help to ensure equal treatment for all. A range of resources are available on the website.

The 1990 Trust
Suite 12
Winchester House
9 Cranmer Road
London SW9 6EJ
Tel: 020 7582 1990
Email: blink1990@blink.org.uk
Web site: www.blink.org.uk

The 1990 Trust provides a range of services from training, research and policy development, to a web site called BLINK (Black Information Link) which contains information on a range of issues and initiatives.

Chinese Mental Health Association
2nd Floor
Zenith House
155 Curtain Road
London EC2A 3QY
Tel: 020 7613 1008
Fax: 020 7739 6577
Web site: www.cmha.org.uk

Chinese Mental Health Association is a registered charity dedicated to serving the Chinese community in the UK. The Association is actively involved in providing direct services, increasing mental health awareness, representing Chinese mental health issues in public forum and raising its profile in our community. A range of resources and information is available on the website.

CAMHS Survey Questionnaires

Questionnaire for Tier 3 Specialist CAMHS Managers

Recording Information

1. How do you define minority ethnic groups?

....

....

....

2. Do you record data about the ethnicity of clients?

☐ No (go to Q6) ☐ Yes (go to Q3)

3. Which source is this data obtained from?

☐ Child ☐ Parent/Carer ☐ Referrer ☐ Other (please specify)

....

4. What type of data do you collect about ethnicity of clients? (tick all relevant boxes)

☐ Country of origin ☐ Language(s) spoken ☐ Religious needs

☐ Dietary requirements ☐ Other (please specify)

....

5a. Is this data used for planning the provision of services?

     □ No (go to Q6)   □ Yes (briefly describe how the data is used)

....

....

....

5b. Tick the box that describes most closely how adequate this data is for service planning.

     □ Very adequate   □ Adequate   □ Don't know

     □ Inadequate   □ Very inadequate

5c. Briefly describe why you think this is the case.

....

....

....

6. What percentage of clients using your service are from minority ethnic groups?

....

7. Do you think this reflects the need for support from your service among local minority ethnic groups?

     □ No (why do you think this is the case?)   □ Yes (how do you assess this?)

     □Don't know

....

....

....

Staff, Training and Support

8. How do you ensure your staff are trained to meet the needs of an ethnically diverse client group?

....
....
....

9. How do you evaluate the value of training and support provided?

....
....
....

10. Does your team include staff from minority ethnic groups?

☐ No (why is that?)

☐ Yes (which positions in your service do they occupy?)

....
....
....

11a. Do you think that your staff would benefit from additional training in this area?

☐ No (go to Q12)   ☐ Yes (go to Q11b)

11b. On which topics?

....

11c. What format would be most useful? (local training events, national training events, written resources and so on)

....
....
....

Service Provision

12a. Do you undertake targeted publicity to inform minority ethnic groups about your services?

    ☐ No (why do you think that is the case?)

    ☐ Yes (please say how you achieve this)

....
....
....

12b. Do you feel your service is able to meet the needs of a culturally diverse population?

    ☐ No (why do you think that is the case?)

    ☐ Yes (how have you achieved this? Provision of specialist services, training, partnerships with community groups and so on)

....
....
....

12c. Have you evaluated the impact of services provided to minority ethnic groups?

    ☐ Yes   ☐ No

13. Do you liase with other agencies that have relevant experience in this field?

    ☐ No (why do you think that is the case?)

    ☐ Yes (please specify agencies and type of contact, statutory/voluntary)

....
....
....

14. Do clients from minority ethnic groups contribute to any aspect of planning and provision of services?

☐ No (why do you think that is the case?)

☐ Yes (please specify the nature of their involvement)

....

....

....

CAMHS Commissioners' Questionnaire

1. How do you define minority ethnic groups?

....

....

....

2. Which sources do you used to obtain profiles of the local minority ethnic population?

....

....

....

3. How is this data used for commissioning CAMHS provision for local minority ethnic groups?

....

....

....

4a. Please indicate on the following scale the extent to which this data is adequate in planning services for minority ethnic groups?

☐ Very adequate   ☐ Adequate   ☐ Don't know

☐ Inadequate   ☐ Very inadequate

4b. In what way is it adequate/inadequate?

....

....

....

5a. Do you undertake an assessment of needs for the local minority ethnic population?

☐ Yes (go to Q5b)   ☐ No (go to Q6)

5b. When was the last assessment undertaken?

....

5c. How was the data used?

....

....

....

6. Do you have up-to-date information about the local minority ethnic population in relation to:

Their awareness about mental health?	☐ Yes	☐ No
Their awareness about mental health services?	☐ Yes	☐ No
Their access to services?	☐ Yes	☐ No
Types of services taken up?	☐ Yes	☐ No
Any discrepancies in types of services taken up?	☐ Yes	☐ No

7. Do you undertake regular reviews of service provision to minority ethnic groups in relation to:

Promotion of mental health?	☐ Yes	☐ No
Identification of mental health problems?	☐ Yes	☐ No
Assessment of mental health problems?	☐ Yes	☐ No
Appropriateness of services to meet needs?	☐ Yes	☐ No
Effectiveness of interventions provided?	☐ Yes	☐ No

8. Do you provide any guidelines to providers about addressing the mental health needs of clients from local minority ethnic groups?

☐ Yes (what are they?)   ☐ No (why is that?)

9. Do you specify requirements, in service specifications and contracts with providers, about provision of services to address the mental health needs of the local minority ethnic population?

☐ Yes (what are they?)   ☐ No (why is that?)

10. Do you use any providers from the voluntary/community sector?

☐ Yes (what are they?)   ☐ No (why is that?)

11. In your view, what would improve the provision of services to address the mental health needs of local minority ethnic groups?

....

....

....

12. How many Tier 3 teams are there in your area?

....

Team name

....

Area covered

....

Team manager

....

Contact number

....

Subject Index

Author Index